Parallel Processing in Information Systems

With Examples and Cases

John Van Zandt

John Wiley & Sons, Inc.
NEW YORK • CHICHESTER • BRISBANE • TORONTO • SINGAPORE

Library of Congress Cataloging-in-Publication Data

Van Zandt, John
  Parallel processing in information systems with examples and cases
/ John Van Zandt.
    p.   cm.
  Includes bibliographical references and index.
  ISBN 0-471-54822-7 (cloth : alk. paper)
    1. Parallel processing (Electronic computers) I. Title.
QA76.58.V36   1992
004'.35–dc20   92-5255
                                                                     CIP

Printed in the United States of America
10 9 8 7 6 5 4 3 2 1

For Billie Jo, Erica, and Darren

About the Author
John W. Van Zandt, Ph.D.

Dr. John Van Zandt is an independent consultant specializing in parallel processing for the scientific and commercial worlds. He has been in the field since 1983 and is a leading expert on parallel processing. He designed and built the Loral LDF-100, one of the first commercially available parallel processors, in 1986. Dr. Van Zandt has also been the director of future systems at Sequent Computer Systems, where he focused on research on new applications of parallel processing and led the team that designed the next-generation Sequent computer system. Prior to that he was the engineering manager at Intel Scientific Computers during the introduction of the iPSC/860.

He founded the parallel processing laboratory at GE Aerospace Labs, which explored applications of parallel and distributed processors. Early in his career, he was a founding member of the UCSD Pascal project, which created a unique programming environment for the first personal computers.

Dr. Van Zandt received his undergraduate and graduate education at the University of California (San Diego). He is a member of the ACM and the IEEE. He has given many invited talks and taught courses at the University of California (San Diego) and Drexel University.

Contents

Preface

Parallel processing technology is currently undergoing a quiet revolution, which will have a dramatic impact on the future of computing. The revolution is happening outside of the academic and research labs. It is being instigated by several computer manufacturers, who are successfully selling parallel processors for use in commercial environments. The most successful and technologically advanced companies are putting these new machines to work as part of their information strategy in their information systems (IS) departments, because parallel processors are providing them with a substantial competitive edge. Key industry analysts, as well as most companies serving the business computing environment, recognize that by the end of the 1990s the majority of computers, from lowly PCs to high-end database servers to supercomputers, will be multiprocessors and parallel processors.

As with all revolutions, speed is important, and inaction can lead to failure. It will be critical over the next five years that business and information systems professionals understand this technology so they can apply it to give their companies a competitive edge in information technology. This book, then, is meant for them.

Information systems professionals and other computer professionals will use this book to understand the basics of the technology that will be affecting their lives in the next few years. They will learn the fundamental principles that are now emerging in parallel processors as the third generation of parallel computers become reality. The book will examine how and why parallel computers will be quickly invading the conventional computing environments.

Management and strategic planners who are trying to understand the information age and how it is affecting them will use the book to gain insight into the capabilities of parallel processors and see examples of the competitive edge they are providing to companies. Only through applying this technology will companies be able to strategically use the information available to them.

Chapter 1: Why Parallel Processing?

This chapter explores reasons and motivations behind parallel processors, covering the limitations on sequential processors and the enabling technologies for parallel processors.

Chapter 2: Classification of Parallel Processors

One of the hardest things to understand is how to categorize and differentiate among all the parallel processors that exist or are being designed. This chapter classifies the parallel processors and exposes the reader to the basic differences and their consequences for the user/programmer.

Chapter 3: Early Generations of Parallel Processors

Parallel processors have been around for 20 years. The first generation was devoted solely to research machines, such as the C.mmp and the Illiac IV. The second generation saw parallel machines being produced and sold by companies, such as the TMC Connection Machine, the BBN Butterfly, and the Intel iPSC/1. Each of these machines is discussed in detail in this chapter. For each machine the focus is on the causes leading to its lack of wide acceptance and how it contributed to the foundation for the third generation.

Chapter 4: The Third Generation—Commercializing Parallel Processing

The third generation of parallel processors is finally establishing itself in the commercial world. This chapter examines some of the latest parallel processors in a series of examples. In each case, the focus is on why the machine is successful in the commercial environment. The Sequent Symmetry 2000 is looked at as the power platform for relational databases, bringing parallel processing and open systems to the information systems market. The MasPar MP-1's role is as an application accelerator. The Intel iPSC/860 is the first parallel computer to achieve true supercomputer performance. Finally, the Teradata DBC/1012 is changing the way companies manage their online information.

Chapter 5: Parallel Processor—New Releases

During 1992, Thinking Machines Corporation and Intel Corporation have released their latest parallel processors, with architectures which will carry through much of the 1990's. These two machines, the TMC CM-5 and the Intel Paragon, will be analyzed to see what the future holds.

Chapter 6: Application Domains

Parallel processors are currently solving a wide range of business problems. This chapter analyzes two case studies: US West NewVector Group and Prudential Securities, both of which have incorporated state-of-the-art parallel processors into their strategic computing environments.

Chapter 7: Programming Parallel Processors

One of the big differences among the parallel processors is the extent to which existing applications can be used unchanged. The challenge is how to write a program (or modify an existing one) that can take advantage of the parallel processing. This chapter gives examples of the two main approaches for writing parallel programs: data partitioning and function partitioning. The languages, tools, and programming environments for parallel processing are described.

Chapter 8: Selecting a Parallel Computer

Now is the time for a company, no matter what size, to start planning and implementing an information strategy incorporating a parallel processor. This chapter covers the basic criteria, both quantitative and qualitative, that should be used to help select a parallel processor.

Chapter 9: The Future of Parallel Processing

The future for parallel processing looks bright. It will be the dominant form of computing by the end of the 1990s. This chapter explores some of the applications that are enabled by this technology, which will give foresighted companies an edge in the information age.

The information age is happening all around us. Retail firms are collecting vast quantities of data regarding buying habits of individual consumers and detecting trends that are happening in different markets worldwide. Financial firms are using computers to monitor news in realtime to be the first with a piece of knowledge that can affect the market. Companies in every business sector are discovering that their competitive edge relies on better utilizing information, and parallel processing is providing the enabling technology.

Lake Oswego, Oregon   JOHN VAN ZANDT

Acknowledgments

Many people helped make this book a reality:

My editors at John Wiley & Sons, Diane Cerra and Terri Hudson, who had faith in the project.

My West Coast editor, Nancy Cisneros, who worked with my rough drafts to create readable text.

David King, who helped get the project off the ground.

Peter Christy of MasPar, Rick Gimbel of Sequent Computer Systems, Wendy Vittori and Joanne Wold of Intel, and Robin Tanchum of Teradata who provided much-needed background information.

John Black of US West and Dr. David Audley of Prudential Securities, who provided me with invaluable information for the case studies in Chapter 6.

All the computer science researchers and entrepreneurs who believed in parallel processing and made it happen.

My wife and children, especially, without whose patience and support it would not have been possible.

Thank you all.
J.V.Z.

Trademark List

- i286, i386, i486, i860, Concurrent File System, Paragon, and iPSC are trademarks of Intel Corporation and its affiliates.
- BBN Butterfly is a trademark of BBN, Inc.
- Connection Machines is a registered trademark, and DataVault, CM-1, CM-2, and CM-5 are trademarks, of Thinking Machines Corporation.
- Ethernet is a trademark of Xerox Corporation.
- IBM is a registered trademark, and MVS, IMS, System 360, and System 370 are trademarks, of International Business Machines Corporation.
- SYSTEMPRO is a trademark of Compaq Computer Corporation.
- nCUBE is a trademark of nCUBE Corporation.
- NeXT is a trademark of NeXT Corporation.
- MasPar is a registered trademark, and MasPar Programming Environment, MasPar Fortran, and MasPar Parallel Application Library are trademarks of MasPar Computer Corporation.
- OSF/1 is a trademark of the Open Software Foundation, Inc.
- POSIX is a trademark of the Institute of Electrical and Electronic Engineers, Inc.
- Sequent, Symmetry, DYNIX, and Balance are registered trademarks of Sequent Computer Systems, Inc.
- Star Trek is a registered trademark and Star Trek: The Next Generation is a trademark of Paramount Pictures.

- DBC/1012 is a trademark of Teradata Corporation.
- TPC, TPC-A, and TPC-B are registered trademarks of Transaction Processing Performance Council.
- UNIX is a registered trademark of AT&T Bell Laboratories.
- VAX is a trademark of Digital Equipment Corporation.
- CAMPUS/800 is a trademark of Alliant Computer Systems Corporation.
- 386/smp and 486/smp are trademarks of Corollary, Inc.
- CRAY and CRAY Y-MP are registered trademarks of CRAY Research, Inc.
- Encore Infinity 90 is a trademark of Encore Computer Corporation.
- KSR1 is a trademark of Kendall Square Research Corporation.
- Computing Surface is a trademark of Meiko Scientific.
- NetFRAME is a registered trademark of NetFRAME Systems, Inc.
- MIServer and Reliant are trademarks of Pyramid Technology Corporation.
- IRISserver and Silicon Graphics are trademarks of Silicon Graphics, Inc.
- Stratus is a registered trademark and XA/R is a trademark of Stratus Computer, Inc.
- SPARCsystem and SPARC are trademarks of SPARC International, Inc.
- ComputeServer and TORQUE are trademarks of Torque Systems, Inc.

List of Figures

1

Why Parallel Processing?

All for one, one for all.
Alexander Dumas, *The Three Musketeers*

In academic circles, parallel processing has been discussed for years. Many experimental machines have been designed; some designs have made their way to production. They are intriguing, but are they applicable to the important tasks that confront businesses every day?

A Competitive Edge

A reporter inside today's most information-advanced companies might write news articles like the ones that follow:

CHICAGO.   The first day of the week-long white sale is over for a large national retailer. Sales information from each of the stores has already started flowing to headquarters. Within an hour after the close of business, all sales data is being processed by the company's new information system. At the heart of it is a parallel processor. Trend information is analyzed, and the computer prints out the major buying patterns. Several items show low sales in the Northeast region but a huge demand in the Midwest.

After reviewing the report, the distribution manager decides that the items noted in the report will sell faster in the Midwest and that it is worth the cost of shipping for customers to get merchandise rather than rainchecks. Concentrating on the Midwest will also help ensure that the inventory will be sold.

Within two hours of the close of business, orders are sent to the stores, and the selected items are loaded onto the nightly trucks that ship the merchandise between stores. By the opening of business the next day, the high-demand goods are in the stores most likely to sell them. The company generates more satisfied customers and more revenue while reducing inventories.

This scenario is possible only because the company was able to collect and process the vast amount of information available to it in a timely way. If the process had taken hours instead of minutes, efficient distribution of the goods could not have happened. Parallel processing offers the opportunity to change the way that companies use the information they have.

NEW YORK.   The chief financial officer of a large multinational corporation walks into an investment firm for his 9 A.M. appointment. The meeting is to discuss placing a portfolio of bonds with the investment firm. He is told by one of the investment bankers that he will get an offer for the placement by 8 A.M. the following morning. The CFO thanks the banker and says he will look forward to the offer. Meanwhile, the bankers start to analyze the opportunity to determine the profit they will get at the various interest rates. Because of the complexity of the transaction, their mainframe computer will be processing for eight hours to perform the necessary calculations. Because of the expense of the mainframe, the computer does double duty: During the day it runs business transactions, so only at night is it freed up to execute this special analysis program.

> The CFO has now shown up for his 10 A.M. appointment with the investment firm across the street. He meets with their investment bankers and explains the opportunity. Here, after he presents the plan, he is given a cup of coffee and told they will have his answer in 10 minutes. This firm has just installed a new parallel processor that can perform the necessary calculations in minutes. And because it is based on microprocessor technology, it is only a fraction of the price of a mainframe. The investment bankers are able to present their offer to the CFO before he is finished with his coffee. He is impressed enough with the service and the offer. He feels this is the right firm to do business with. The investment firm, through information technology and parallel processing, has been able to generate customer satisfaction and revenue.

Untapped Information

Current estimates are that less than 5 percent of a company's information is online. In the information age, a key strategic asset for a company is its information: the data about the business and the knowledge and processes that comprise the company. To be competitive, companies must capture and use as much of this information as possible. This demand for information will accelerate the consumption of computer power. The information explosion will not grow in a linear fashion. Each new piece of information will be associated not just with one existing piece of information but with many existing pieces. This leads to an exponential growth of linkages, which will require an equivalent growth of computing capability.

So the question is: Can we get there from here? In terms of computing power, the answer is: It is already happening, but not in the way you expect.

The Rise of Parallel Computers

Most computers today are *sequential* computers. That is, they are capable of doing only one task at a time. Because of time-sharing, the computer may appear to be doing multiple tasks simultaneously, but in reality the computer is simply switching between the tasks frequently. Because of fundamental limits in computing technology, as described below, the speed of a sequential computer is going to reach a performance limit.

Parallelism through Arithmetic

When parallel processing is mentioned, most computer and information systems professionals think of experimental machines, possibly scientific supercomputers, that are useful for only a handful of applications. It has not always been that way. The first simple example of the early value placed on parallel processing comes from the dawn of computing, when John von Neumann (the father of computing) and his colleagues were designing one of the first computers, the ENIAC. There were valuable discussions on the need for parallelism.[1] The machine was designed so that the arithmetic would be performed in parallel instead of serially—bit by bit. It is worthwhile to remember that people compute serially, so that making the arithmetic unit work 40 bits at a time was a break from tradition. Today, no one thinks about having computers operate serially on the bits. Everyone expects that computer arithmetic will be done in parallel. Value is placed on computers that perform arithmetic more in parallel than others do; thus, a 16-bit computer is not as good as a 32-bit computer. Here, the number of bits signify the parallelism in the arithmetic of the computer.

Parallelism through I/O

In the 1950s, computers could do only one thing at a time. When a computer was executing a program and needed to read a card or write to the printer, the program would be suspended while the I/O operation took place. The computer's processing unit had to be actively involved in the execution of the I/O.

The early IBM 7090 series computers were so expensive that users tried their best to keep the computer processing programs. Although the computers could have a card reader and printer directly attached to them, users preferred instead for programs to do all of their I/O to magnetic tape, which was much faster and thus caused the processor to suspend the program for shorter periods. To accommodate the need for card input and printed output, users set up their own "parallel processors." They read their cards into an IBM 1401, which wrote the card images to tape; then the tape was carried over to the IBM 7090 and loaded. The 7090 then read the tape, executed the programs, and wrote the printer files back to the tape, which was again carried back to the IBM 1401 for printing. This allowed the two computers to be used in parallel—a practice sometimes called "sneaker parallelism."

In the 1960s, computers were created that had separate processors for program execution and I/O. This enabled computers to continue processing programs while the I/O operation was being performed. An early example of this is the IBM 360/44, whose *channel processors* were capable of executing strings of commands, called *channel programs,* concurrently with the continued execution of the main program. This improved the throughput of the computer. It required some special software to take advantage of the capability, but the gain in throughput was worth the effort.

Parallelism through Shared Resources

As early as 1963, some computers were built that could share some of the resources. The processor was not the dominant cost in even the earliest computers. I/O devices and memory accounted for more of the cost than the processor. Computer manufacturers recognized this fact and produced computers that had up to three processors that could share these more expensive resources. They discovered that the performance of these computers would actually go up (although they wouldn't scale linearly). The IBM 360/67 and the Burroughs B6000 series were built this way. The IBM 360/67 could have up to three processors.[2] The Burroughs B6700 could have up to three processors and three I/O processors, in any configuration.[3] Nobody thought of these as parallel processors, and they were readily accepted by the commercial data processing community.

The Many Faces of Parallel Processing

Many approaches exist to the realization of parallel processing. A popularly held definition of a parallel processor is one that is *designed to execute a single program at a time, with all processors working on some aspect of the same program.*

This canonical perception of a parallel processor is too narrow. Following are four common implementations of parallel processing that exist today:

Implementation #1: Multiprogramming

The capability (with one or more processors) to concurrently execute more than one process (program) at a time. The processes (programs) do not necessarily execute simultaneously, but instead take turns getting parts of themselves executed. Most operating systems have this capability today.

Implementation #2: The multiprocessor

A computer composed of more than one processor, as shown in Figure 1-1. Typically, each processor executes a different program with little interaction between the processors. One memory system is shared among the multiple processors (see Figure 1-1). Examples are the Sequent Symmetry 2000 series and the Compaq SystemPro.

Implementation #3: The multicomputer

A computer composed of more than one processor-memory pair, as shown in Figure 1-2. Whereas with a multiprocessor there is only one memory system, in a multicomputer each processor has its own memory. The processors com-

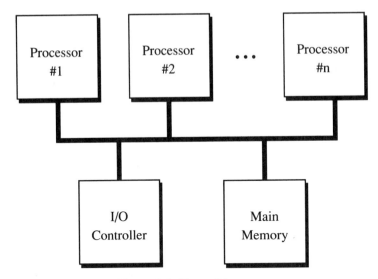

Figure 1-1. *The multiprocessor*

municate by passing messages over the interconnection network (which can be a bus, a local area network, or a proprietary network). Examples are the nCUBE line of computers, the Intel iPSC/860, and the Teradata DBC/1012.

Implementation #4: The special-case parallel processor

A multiprocessor or multicomputer that is designed for optimizing the execution of one program at a time. This is a special case. The difference lies in the limitation that a parallel processor normally can execute only one program at a time. The Thinking Machines Corporation CM-2 fits into this category.

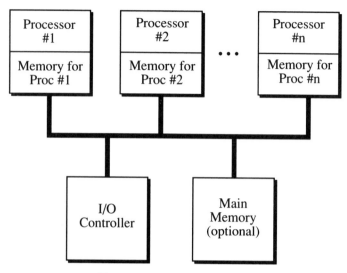

Figure 1-2. *The multicomputer*

Why Single Processors Will Run Out of Steam

Computer scientists believe that parallel processing will dominate computer technologies because sooner or later (and it looks like sooner) the performance of a single, stand-alone processor is going to peak. The primary cause is the speed of light. Electronic devices can be placed only so close together. The signals must travel a distance (for example, between the processing unit and the memory), and the speed at which the signals travel is governed by the speed of light, 300,000 kilometers per second. At the speed of light, an electric signal travels about 12 inches per nanosecond. The distance between the memory and the processor might be a large fraction of this distance. This puts a limit on the clock rate of a processor and therefore a limit on its performance—and clock rates for computers are already approaching 1 nanosecond per cycle.

The second reason is the economics. It is more expensive to build a single fast processor than to build several slow ones. The car industry provides an analogy. Sports cars that go 150 mph are rare and expensive, but a sports car that can go 200 mph (33

ATTENTION KMART SHOPPERS

What does a store do when a $29.97 Christmas doll doesn't sell? Get stuck with 36,000 of them? Not if you are Kmart.

During the weekend after Thanksgiving of 1989, that is the situation Kmart found itself in; lots of dolls and no buyers. But because of a parallel processor that the company had bought, it was able to identify the problem and to guide the stores through a series of price cuts, which sold all but a few dolls before Christmas, and with no markdown above 25 percent off.

That computer uses its parallel processors to sift through the sales data each day from the company's stores, spot the winners and losers, and help take corrective action. That same Christmas season, the computer discovered a fast-selling tree ornament, which was able to be ordered in enough time to get more. Just those two product moves increased the bottom line at Kmart by $250,000.

The computer is a DBC/1012 from Teradata Corporation. It is composed of 254 Intel microprocessors (the same chips used in PCs), which work together on large database applications. The computer is specially designed for database work. It attaches to standard mainframes and offloads them from this normally time-consuming task.

Kmart President Joseph E. Antonini has credited the Teradata machine with significantly increasing profits for that Christmas season. For coming years, Kmart now has a better idea of what sells and at what price.

Source: Larry Armstrong, "Teradata Gets Magic From A Gang Of Microchips," *BusinessWeek,* November 26, 1990.

percent faster) will cost more than 33 percent more. The price per mph increases exponentially as the maximum mph increases. In computers, the cost of a single Cray-2 processor is much more expensive than the cost of a standard computer.

The Enabling Technologies

Driving this change in computing fundamentals is the confluence of two main technology streams: commodity hardware, in the form of microprocessors, memories, and disks; and commodity software, in the form of open systems. The term *commodity hardware* refers to computer parts that are produced in large quantities and are sold with low profit margins because of the number of producers. Microprocessors are a good example of a commodity. An *open system* denotes a computer that is not based on a proprietary software interface. That is, software from other vendors can be used to increase the functionality and performance of the computer. Thus, the application software is relatively independent of the hardware platform. This leads to commodity software.

In the past, better performance meant greater cost. It is interesting that the next quantum leap in performance required in the information age will come about through less costly technology.

Commodity Microprocessors, Memories, and Disks

One of the distinct advantages that parallel processors have over traditional computers is their reliance on commodity components. The main subsystems—the processor, the memory subsystem, and the mass-storage subsystem—are all composed of PC- and workstation-class components. This means that a parallel processor can have the advantage of price/performance at levels similar to PCs while achieving performance equivalent to (or greater than) mainframes and supercomputers.

The advances that microprocessors have made in the past 15 years are a classic example of this effect. The first microprocessor was developed in the early 1970s. The first PC was shipped in the mid-1970s. The first PCs were not much more powerful than programmable calculators, but in the intervening time, the performance has grown at a compound rate of almost 100 percent per year. Microprocessors of the mid-1990s will be as powerful as the first Cray supercomputer, the Cray-1. By the end of the 1990s, Intel predicts, there will be a microprocessor as powerful as the Cray-2, or roughly 25 times as powerful as an IBM 3090.

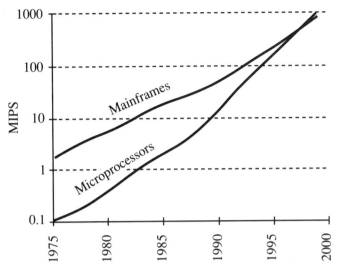

Figure 1-3. *Microprocessor vs. mainframe performance growth*

As the graph in Figure 1-3 shows, the performance of microprocessors is increasing more rapidly than that of mainframes or
supercomputers.

SYNTHETIC PROGRAMS AND BENCHMARKS

A *synthetic program* (also called a *synthetic benchmark*) is a program constructed specifically to benchmark computer systems. It is
constructed, usually statistically, to model a class of applications.
The program itself does not actually perform the application, but
it has computation and I/O characteristics that are similar to those
of the real applications. This is discussed in greater detail in Chapter 7.

While the foregoing graph was measured in million of in-structions per second (MIPS), that is not as meaningful as a more application-based benchmark. The TP-1 benchmarks are standard synthetic programs, which are used in the information systems industry to measure the overall performance of a com-puter on transaction processing applications. Figure 1-4 shows the performance of computers over the past five years, com-paring microprocessor-based computers with traditional main-frames. Note that the performance of the microprocessor-based systems is increasing faster using this metric as well. The other factor influencing technology trends is the economics of building and manufacturing computers. Mainframe technology is expen-sive. Mainframes and supercomputers cost almost 10 times the price of microprocessor-based computers. Figure 1-5 shows the price per transaction/second (TPS) of computers.

And so, we see that the next leap in information-processing systems will come from technology that is substantially less costly than its predecessors and based on commodity hardware. The same trend is happening in the software arena with open sys-tems.

Open Systems

The other change that is happening in the computer arena is the increasing importance of open systems. The term *open systems,*

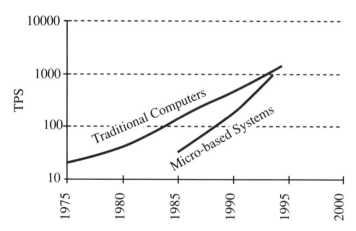

Figure 1-4. *Microprocessor vs. mainframe TP-1 performance growth*

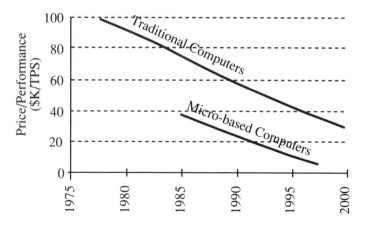

Figure 1-5. *Price/performance of microcomputers vs. mainframe computers*

which had meant running the UNIX operating system, now has a different meaning: conforming to standards that allow the interoperability of computing platforms, as well as the independence of the software applications from any one company's proprietary interfaces. For example, the POSIX standards define a set of interfaces between application programs and the operating system such that an application conforming to the standards can run with only recompilation on any computer with an operating system offering the POSIX interface.

As standards for hardware and software have developed, it has become easier for users to switch between competing vendors. This has enabled companies that were hooked to proprietary vendors to embrace newer technologies. Today, most commercial parallel processors embrace a wide range of standards, from microprocessor and bus standards to operating system interfaces and communication protocol standards. The key advantage of this to a user is the opening up of a wider range of capabilities than exists with any one vendor.

The open systems concept is so successful because it creates standards that a large body of users share, increasing the total available market, which in turn supports the development of additional capabilities. The PC marketplace is the best example of this. If each PC manufacturer had its own operating system, thereby requiring applications to be rewritten for each system, the market would be fragmented into dozens of segments, each with maybe only a million users. Each segment would have its unique set of applications, but none would have a complete set. But since all of the PC vendors developed to a standard, running a standard operating system (MS-DOS), the marketplace grew to 40 million PCs. This meant that application providers could focus their attention on development for one operating system.

This works to advantage for both vendors and users. Vendors like to see a large market in which they can grow and compete; this supports a large investment in R&D. Users get to pick from a larger capability set than would exist with any one vendor.

Conclusion

Summary

Companies are being plunged into the information age and are being required to utilize ever-increasing amounts of information in order to remain competitive.

Companies are just beginning to break the surface of the pool of information that comprises their businesses. Managing that overwhelming amount of information will require computers many times more powerful than today's machines. The single-processor computer is rapidly becoming a thing of the past, because of hardware limits of the technology and cost/performance considerations. The only way to achieve cost-effective high-performance computing is through parallelism. An interesting twist is that because of parallelism, the technologies used to construct the high-performance information computers of tomorrow will be the same ones that are used in PCs and workstations today: commodity microprocessors, memories, and disks.

Key Points

1. To be more competitive in the future, companies are going to have to develop new ways to capture and utilize the information in their companies.
2. Parallel processors come in many forms, but all share the ability to execute an application using more than one processor.
3. Parallel processors will be the dominant form of large-scale computing in the coming years.

4. Because of the construction of parallel processors out of the commodity technologies used in PCs and workstations, parallel processors provide large price/performance advantages over traditional computers.

5. Open systems and the standards they entail will enable more rapid absorption of parallel processing technology into the mainstream of information systems.

6. Basic parallel processing concepts have been around for three decades, but only recently have they been converted into commercial advantage.

References

1. A. W. Burks, H. H. Goldstine, and J. von Neumann, "Preliminary Discussion of the Logical Design of an Electronic Computing Instrument, Part II," *Datamation,* vol. 8, October 1962, pp. 36–41.

2. B. W. Arden, B. A. Galler, T. C. O'Brien, and F. H. Westervelt, "Program and Addressing Structure in a Time-Sharing Environment," *Journal of the ACM,* vol. 13, January 1966, pp. 1–16.

3. Burroughs Corporation, *B6700 Information Processing System Reference Manual* (Detroit, 1969).

2

Classification of Parallel Processors

Variety's the very spice of life,
That gives it all its flavour.

Cowper, *The Task, II*

When one first surveys the field of parallel processors, the wide variety of machines can be overwhelming. With single-processor systems, the most obvious differences are among the instruction sets (the set of commands that tell a computer what to do). With knowledge and experience of one single-processor computer system, it is easy to understand a different one. Comparing them is sometimes more aesthetic than analytical; there is no doubt that any of the single-processor computers can do an application.

Contrast this with parallel processors, where the first question is usually, "Can the computer perform the application?" Though this question has historical merit, since the early parallel processors were little more than experiments, we shall see that the capabilities of parallel processors have increased to the point that now the question is one of efficiency: "How well can the application perform on the machine, and how easy it is to create the application?"

Classification Schemes

Conversations about parallel processors can quickly turn into catalogs of features such as single instruction-stream multiple data-stream (SIMD), multiple instruction-stream multiple data-stream (MIMD), data parallel programming, interconnection networks, hypercubes, and message latencies. On the surface, at least, each machine seems to be totally different from the others. It is difficult to determine how to compare machines when they seem to have nothing in common. The important first step toward solving this dilemma is to develop a categorization scheme that shows the fundamental similarities and important differences among what appear to be vastly different machines.

Many categorization schemes have been proposed in the literature.[1,2] The one used here is based on ideas first proposed by M. J. Flynn,[3] who classifies machines by the characteristics most visible to the programmer. These ideas are further refined by explaining the characteristics in terms of the fundamental operations unique to parallel processors.

Fundamental Differences

The fundamental operational difference between sequential and parallel processors is the coordination that must occur between the processors in a parallel machine.

In a sequential processor, the programmer is concerned only about the algorithmic correctness of the program. At any point in the program, the programmer needs to think only about the task currently at hand. Nothing is happening behind the programmer's back. Not so in a parallel processor. Two additional operations must be considered: communication and synchronization. These operations are shown in Figure 2-1.

Communication

When multiple processors are working together to execute a program, they must communicate—pass information back and forth between the processors. If there is no communication, then the processors must be working on different programs. The information can be transferred in many different ways (messages transmitted between processors, data put into a shared memory, special interrupts), but it is all part of communication.

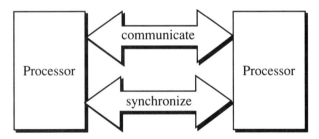

Figure 2-1. *Parallel processors must communicate and synchronize.*

Synchronization

The second important operation in a parallel processor is synchronization. If two processors are working on a single program, each one, at various points in its execution, must be cognizant of the state of the other.

Think of an assembly line, which is one analogy for a parallel processor. If two workers on an assembly line have no knowledge of the progress of each other's work, then there will be a malfunction at some point. The work that is being performed by the first worker in the assembly line will not be able to be passed on to the second. Or, the first one will get too far ahead of the second. Or the second one will be so far behind that the work gets out of order. The list could go on and on.

Basically, the two workers on the assembly line must stay in synch. Without synchronization, the system will fail.

Therefore, we will classify the parallel processors on their style of communication and synchronization. Those are the only dimensions that have underlying fundamental importance.

Equivalence of Parallel Processors

One of the truly amazing characteristics of parallel processors is that while they are constructed with an incredibly diverse set of basic architectures, processor types, memory speeds, and other features, the overall performance of each of the machines on actual applications is within a factor of two to three of each other. None of the machines has demonstrated a tenfold performance advantage over other machines with a similar technology basis (built out of the same generation of parts). This leads to the conclusion that there exists some yet undiscovered truth about performance capability that is architecture-independent. This can be thought of as the physics of computation. In the same way that the physical properties of building materials limit the height of a building, the electrical properties of an existing technology limit the performance—no matter how the pieces are put together.

Another dimension, which has received an inordinate amount of attention in the literature, is interconnection networks. Historically, parallel processor research journals have been filled with papers on different topologies for interconnecting processors. This esoteric topic has little, if anything, to do with the fundamentals of parallel processing. As an analogy, if a book on transportation systems focused on the layout of the roads and how many intersections were on an average street instead of discussing cars, trains, or planes, it might be mathematically intriguing, but the majority of the users would not be interested. So it is with interconnection networks. However, since they are such an ever-present topic during discussions on parallel processors, they will be covered here.

MIMD

The classification scheme described by Flynn partitions parallel processors into two main groups. The first major class of parallel processors is called multiple instruction-stream multiple data-stream (MIMD, pronounced "mim-dee"). This refers to the case where each processor executes its own program (each has its own set of instructions) and each executes that program on different pieces of data. The processors within this class of machine communicate and synchronize based on asynchronous messages. That is, their programs must contain instructions that cause them to send and receive messages, but since the timing of the arrival of these messages is not knowable by a process, they are asynchronous: There are no architecturally mandated times for the synchronization to occur.

Going back to the assembly-line analogy, assume that each worker has a different task to perform. In order for the workers to perform together smoothly and efficiently, the workers on the assembly line must get together before they start work and agree on a set of hand signals and verbal codes, which compose the communication and synchronization that the workers use.

LIBRARY AUTOMATION EMBRACES PARALLEL PROCESSING

One of the largest classes of users of information consists of libraries. Their role in collecting, organizing, and disseminating information puts them at the forefront of computer technology. And because of their reliance on public funding, they are always looking for very cost-effective technology.

These two drives come together in parallel processing. Many library systems throughout the world (e.g., the City of Paris public library system and the National Library of China in Beijing) base their online catalog on parallel processors. Parallel processing provides a library system with the ability to meet current performance needs economically while being able to accommodate growth in the future. This is because parallel processors can be upgraded by simply adding processors and memory boards. This is in stark contrast to traditional computers, where an upgrade meant moving aside the old computer and bringing in a brand-new one. The cost of upgrading a parallel processor is only a fraction of a traditional upgrade.

The multi-user database applications that are fundamental to library uses are ideal matches for parallel processing. Since each user is doing an independent search through the library catalog system, the multiple processors can be allocated to different users, giving almost perfectly linear speedup over a single processor.

Source: Gene Robinson, "Technologies to Facilitate Access," *Library Journal*, February 1, 1989.

In the same way, the MIMD programmer must plan the points in the program where the independent processors must exchange information to stay synchronized in order to get the job done.

Within this class of parallel processors, two subclasses exist. The first consists of the shared-memory MIMD machines, exemplified by the Sequent Symmetry 2000.[4] The second is the class of distributed-memory machines, exemplified by the Intel Hypercube (iPSC/860).[5] These subclasses are distinguished by their method of communication, which is a direct product of the relationship between the processors and the memory.

Shared Memory

In a shared-memory machine (more accurately referred to as a shared address space), the same memory locations are shared by all the processors. Figure 2-2 shows the functional diagram of the Sequent Symmetry/2000, the prototypical shared-memory computer system.

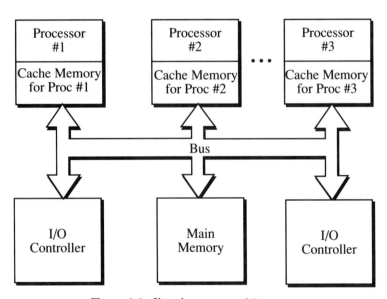

Figure 2-2. *Shared-memory multiprocessor*

Each processor can read or write the same information in memory. That is, any location in memory is readable and writable by all of the processors. This is how both synchronization and communication occur in this class of parallel processor.

It would be as if the assembly-line workers had a large blackboard that everyone could see, and each worker communicated by reading, writing, and erasing information on the blackboard. In Figure 2-2, the bus is used by each of the processors and by the I/O controllers to read and write information into the main memory.

Coordinating which processor is writing a given memory location is up to the programmer. In shared-memory computer systems, special instructions are provided that allow the programmer to guarantee that the reading and writing is done in an orderly (and predictable) fashion. For some applications where unpredictability is required, two processors are allowed to write the same location at the same time, with the result being totally nondeterministic. This is a small but interesting set of applications.[6]

The *cache memory* for these processors is an optimization that improves the performance of the computer without changing the basic shared-memory architecture. The cache holds data that the processor is currently using; this lets the processor avoid always having to read and write the main memory (which is slower than using data in the cache). The hardware of the system makes sure that the information in the cache is consistent with what is in main memory—the cache is invisible to the programmer.

In the shared-memory machine, processors communicate by placing information into the shared memory, where each processor can see it. This communication mechanism is combined with synchronization methods to allow the processors to coordinate who can write where in the memory.

Distributed Memory

In a distributed-memory machine, each processor has its own memory; memory is not shared. Processors communicate by sending messages to each other. Figure 2-3 shows the functional block diagram of the Intel iPSC/860,[7] the canonical distributed-memory computer. The I/O controllers are connected only through

▼

SUPERLINEARITY: WHERE 1 + 1 = 3?

One interesting result of shared-memory nondeterminism is called *superlinearity*. That is, the proportional increase in the performance is greater than the proportional increase in the number of processors. For example, a 20-processor system might exhibit increased performance by a factor of 100 over a single processor on a certain problem. A substantial amount of investigation revealed that when this has occurred, the algorithms in use were taking advantage of nondeterminism in a way that improved performance. In one case, the sequential version of a program stepped through an array from index 1 to 1000, doing what in physics is called a particle-in-cell problem. In the parallel version, updates to the cells (which were in shared memory) happened randomly. The algorithm relied on convergence of the problem, which happened quicker in the random case. It turned out that if the sequential version was modified to use a random index, the sequential version also performed faster, and the superlinearity vanished.

Fundamentally, superlinearity is not actually possible. However, parallel processors have been able to shed light on new algorithms for problem solving.

---

individual processors; they cannot be connected directly to the interconnection network. Computers of this type usually have hundreds or thousands of processors. While this provides more raw processing power, the I/O doesn't scale as easily and programming is not as simple as for the shared-memory machines. The Intel iPSC/860 has up to 128 processors. The nCUBE 2 computer, with a similar architecture, has up to 8192 processors.

The analogy in the assembly-line case is that each worker communicates with the other workers by writing notes on sheets of paper and passing them to co-workers. The effect is the same as with the shared memory, only here the communication takes longer.

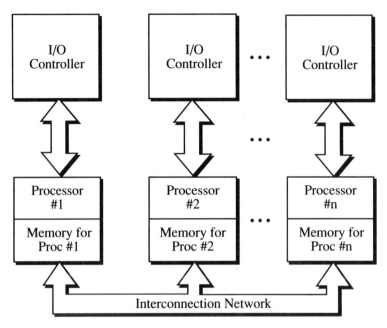

Figure 2-3. *Distributed-memory multiprocessor*

The programmer develops algorithms that allow the work to be partitioned among the processors. Communication and synchronization occur by means of sending messages among the processors.

SIMD

The other major class of parallel processors consists of the single instruction-stream, multiple data-stream machines (SIMD, pronounced "sim-dee"). These machines carry out synchronization implicitly: All processors execute the same instruction at the same time, but each processor uses a different piece of data. It is like a crew of rowers: The drummer strikes a beat, and all the rowers pull in unison. In a SIMD machine, a control processor issues one instruction, and all the processors execute the instruction.

Figure 2-4 shows the functional block diagram of a typical SIMD parallel processor. Each processor has its own local memory. The control processor is responsible for issuing the instructions, which all processors execute at the same time. Today's

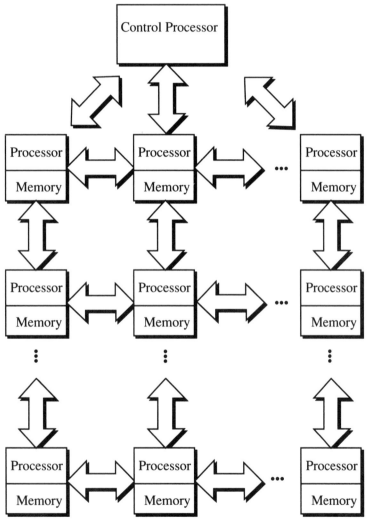

Figure 2-4. *SIMD machine*

SIMD computers are constructed with thousands of processors. This is possible because the regularity and simplicity of each of the processor/memory pairs makes it easy to implement many of them on a single VLSI chip. For example, the CM-2 has up to 65536 processors, with 16 processors per chip.

Synchronization occurs implicitly, because each processor knows exactly where in the program all the other processors are, since they are executing the same instruction. Synchronization does not need to be provided explicitly as it does in a MIMD machine, where each processor is doing its own thing.

The Thinking Machines Corporation's (TMC) Connection Machine is a classic example of this type of machine. So far, all SIMD machines have been built with distributed memories (see Figure 2-5); that is, each processor has its own memory. Communication is accomplished by sending messages (data) from one processor to another (just as in the distributed-memory MIMD machines). There is no fundamental reason for not building a SIMD with a

	Shared-Memory	**Distributed-Memory**
SIMD		CM-1, CM-2 (Thinking Machines Corporation) MP-1 (MasPar) DAP (Active Memory Technology)
MIMD	Symmetry 2000 (Sequent) T-Series (Pyramid) MultiMax (Encore) NCR 3000	iPSC/860 (Intel) nCUBE 2 (nCUBE) T2000 (BBN) DBC/1012 (Teradata)

Figure 2-5. *Table of machine classes*

shared memory (or shared address space); this means that some-time in the future, some computer scientist will propose and build one!

Interconnection Networks

A significant amount of academic effort has been spent arguing over the best way to hook up parallel processors. At one time, the theory was that the interconnection methodology would make a dramatic difference in the performance of the machine. This turned out to be wrong for several reasons. Although communication is important, the critical factor is the ratio of communication to computation. In a parallel program, if a large amount of work gets performed for each message that gets sent or received by a processor, then the program exhibits good parallelism. If, on the other hand, communication dominates computation, then the program performs poorly. In an assembly-line analogy, if workers spend most of their time communicating and little time doing work, then the assembly line is very inefficient. What has been discovered over the past 10 years, by working with real parallel processors, is that the programmer controls the communication/computation ratio. Any program that can be parallelized can have its ratio adjusted with little difficulty. This means that the program can be made to fit the communication speed. An example of this is the Intel iPSC family of computers. From 1985 to 1990, processor performance improved by a factor of 20 (from the Intel 286 to the Intel i860 microprocessors), while the communication speed was held constant. The same programs ran well on all versions of the machine, with only small modifications. The moral is that communication speed by itself is not the most significant factor determining performance. The effort spent on finding optimal interconnection networks was in vain.

Interconnection networks were also investigated for expansibility. It is widely known that a single bus will not scale to thousands of processors. So a search was conducted to find the best interconnection network for thousands of processors. "Best" in this context was not well understood. Most of the research focused on measuring either *latency* (the time it takes for a message to traverse the path from one processor to another) or *bandwidth* (the number of simultaneous messages that can be sent). Ease of manufacture and cost were usually not considered, even though these are some of the most important issues when actually building a system.

What follows are descriptions of the different types of interconnection networks. Remember that even though the sales people like to talk about them, they have little bearing on the machine performance (and certainly should not be used to differentiate the machines from one another).

Buses

The simplest of all is the *bus*. A bus allows exactly one message to be communicated at a time. One processor can send a message to one or many other processors. Sending to all processors is called *broadcasting*. This is a useful function in some types of programs, so with all interconnection networks, computer designers worry about how easy it is to do a broadcast.

On a bus, the mechanism to control who has access to the bus is determined in many ways. Sometimes the bus is time-multiplexed, so that each processor is allocated a certain time to send messages. In a Sequent Symmetry system, the bus uses a rotating priority scheme, where the processors race to see who can get to the bus first, and ties are broken via a priority scheme. The priorities are rotated so that no processor is *starved* (deprived of access to the bus).

In other schemes, a write token is passed among the processors, and only the processor with the write token is allowed to send a message on the bus.

Rings

Ring networks are another approach to interconnecting more than one processor. All of the processors are connected as in Figure 2-6. A message travels from one processor to another following the ring until it arrives at the destination processor. The advantage of this approach is that each processor must deal with only two wires. This means that the number of processors can

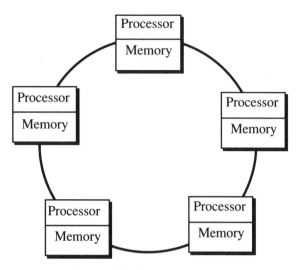

Figure 2-6. *Ring-based system*

be increased without changing the network (without adding new wires to other processors already in the network). The disadvantage of this approach is the length of time it takes to send a message between two processors. In the worst case, a message has to travel all the way around the ring. For small networks this is not a problem. For networks of hundreds of processors, this is a more significant time period and causes changes in the *granularity* (communication/computation ratio) of the processing.

Hypercubes

One of the most-studied forms of interconnection is the *hypercube*, which is a kind of multidimensional geometrical structure (a hypercube in three dimensions is simply a cube). Figure 2-7 shows a hypercube configuration for an eight-processor system. The corners of the cube are the processors, and the edges of the cube are the interconnections between the processors. In this network, a message sent from processor 0 to processor 7 travels first on segment A, then on segment B, and finally on segment C.

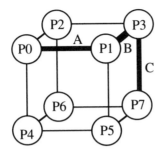

Figure 2-7. *Eight-node hypercube network*

When 2^n processors are interconnected, the resulting structure is an *n*-dimensional hypercube, in which each processor is directly connected to *n* other processors. A four-dimensional hypercube, containing 16 nodes, is shown in Figure 2-8.

The advantage of a hypercube interconnection is that the number of segments that a message travels on grows only logarithmically with the number of processors. Thus, the longest path for a 2048-processor system is 11 segments ($\log_2 2048$). The longest path for a million-processor system is only 20 segments ($\log_2 1,048,576$).

The Intel iPSC family of computers, the nCUBE, and the TMC Connection Machine are all based on this style of interconnect.

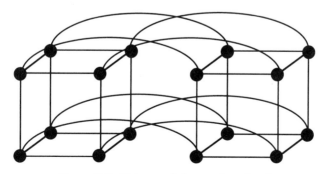

Figure 2-8. *Sixteen-node hypercube network*

Note that the iPSC and the nCUBE are both MIMD computers, while the TMC Connection Machine is a SIMD computer.

One of the problems with this type of network is that since the number of segments coming into and going out of each processor varies with the total number of processors in the system, the system must be built with the maximum configuration in mind. If you want the system to scale to 4000 processors, then you must build all the systems with 12 segments, even though in a small eight-processor system, for example, only three segments would be used for each processor. This causes an additional expense burden for smaller systems, which can lead to their being noncompetitive in price/performance.

Meshes

A mesh is exactly what it sounds like. It looks like a screen, where each processor is connected to its four neighbors, as shown in Figure 2-9. William Daly and Chuck Seitz discovered in 1988 that if one tries to optimize the use of the wires in a system, the hypercube was not the most efficient configuration. They calculated that a mesh was the best structure to fulfill this requirement. One advantage of a mesh is that each processor has only four segments connecting it to its neighbors. This means that the same part can be used no matter how big the parallel processor, as opposed to a hypercube, where the larger the number of processors, the more interconnections each must have. This makes the manufacturing process much easier for the mesh.

Other Interconnection Schemes

As can be seen in Figure 2-10, the number of methods of interconnecting processors appears limited only by one's imagination. Each of these networks has some interesting feature: It may match the communication style of a particular algorithm (such as how data is optimally moved to calculate a fast Fourier transform); it may be redundant; it may have a particularly easy method of computing addressing paths; and so on.

Take, for instance, the tree network shown in Figure 2-10a. This network has the advantage of being able to handle divide-and-conquer problems very efficiently. In this problem-solving

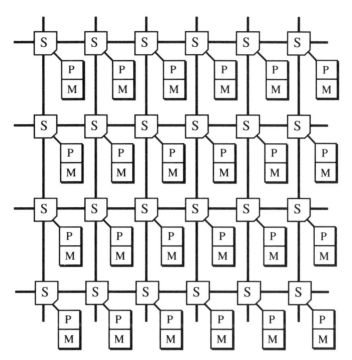

Figure 2-9. *Mesh interconnection*

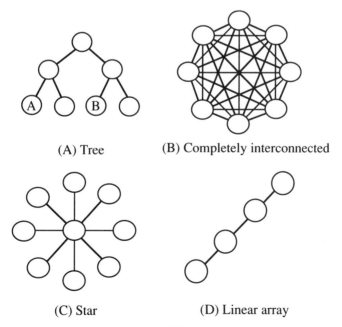

(A) Tree

(B) Completely interconnected

(C) Star

(D) Linear array

Figure 2-10. *Other networks*

approach, the problem is divided among two or more processors, after which the subproblems are again divided among two or more processors, and so on until the subproblems get small enough to be computable or the number of levels in the tree runs out. The answers are then passed up the tree and merged at each step. The communication structure represented by the tree exactly matches the solution methodology. This makes for an optimal communication structure. The disadvantage is that for problems whose solution does not map this way, the communication structure can be highly inefficient. For example, a problem that required significant communication between nodes A and B would not be optimally represented.

Dataflow Computers

The classification schemes covered so far encompass all of the currently available commercial parallel computer systems. They also cover the majority of research machines that have never made it beyond paper designs. However, one style of parallel processor that is difficult to categorize is the *dataflow* processor.[8] This style of machine is based on a unique programming model. Whereas the MIMD machines view synchronization and communication as distinct processes that define the parallelism, a dataflow machine merges the concept of synchronization and communication.

In a dataflow machine, the program is defined as a set of tasks (such as single instructions or subroutines). Each task is independent of the others, in that its execution can proceed as soon as its input data is available. It affects only other tasks that need its output.

A simple example of this is an *instruction-level dataflow*. In Figure 2-11, the statement

$$A = B * C + D * E$$

is shown, based on the dependencies of the input and the output.

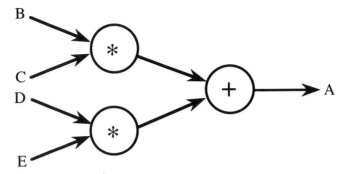

Figure 2-11. *Dataflow processing*

Heterogeneous Multiprocessing

One type of multiple-processor system that is becoming more visible is the *heterogeneous multiprocessor*. Unlike parallel processors, where the processors are fundamentally interchangeable, the heterogeneous multiprocessor has two or more different types of processors, each usually specialized for specific purposes. For example, the NeXT computer actually has two separate processors: one for executing the application program and one for creating the sounds (like music and speech). In programming this machine, the user can actually write separate programs for each processor. Coordination between the processors is left up to the programmer.

Superscalar

The *superscalar* processor is not a true parallel processor. Whereas a parallel processor executes essentially multiple streams of instructions (or data), a superscalar processor provides a clever way of executing a standard, nonparallel program. It recognizes when instructions in the single stream can be executed together. In this way, it optimizes execution of a program rather than performing as a true parallel processor.

An example of this is the execution of the high-level language statement $A = B * C + D * E$. A sequential processor multiplies

$B * C$ first, $D * E$ second, and then adds the intermediate results from the multiplies last. A superscalar processor might have two multiply units, so it would be capable of executing both of the multiplies simultaneously. The superscalar machine would recognize this (either at compile time or at run time), execute the multiplies simultaneously, then perform the add, thus executing the instruction stream in two cycles instead of the sequential three cycles.

Summary

The most straightforward classification scheme for parallel processors is based on the style of synchronization and communication that coordinates the processors in each machine. The two main classes of parallel processors are SIMD and MIMD computers. All commercially available parallel processors fall into one of these classes. Each of these classes is further subdivided by the communication methodology.

The interconnection networks that connect the memories and the processors are not very relevant to the classification of the parallel processors, even though a significant amount of research has gone into this area. The type of interconnection network is not an indicator of machine superiority.

Key Points

1. The majority of parallel processors can be categorized as one of two main types, either MIMD or SIMD.
2. Parallel processors are different from sequential processors because of the added complexity of managing the communication and synchronization between the multiplicity of processors.
3. The primary difference among parallel processors is the programming model that the parallel processor presents to the user. The programming model is the way in which communication and synchronization must be expressed.
4. The interconnection network used to connect the processors together (or to connect the processors and the memory) is not the primary differentiator among machines—it is of secondary concern.

References

1. D. B. Skillicorn, "A Taxonomy for Computer Architectures," *Computer,* November 1988, pp. 46–57.

2. S. Dasgupta, "A Hierarchical Taxonomic System for Computer Architectures," *Computer,* March 1990, pp. 64–74.

3. M. J. Flynn, "Very High-Speed Computing Systems," *Proceedings of the IEEE,* vol. 54, December 1966, pp. 901–909.

4. Sequent Computer Systems, Inc., *Symmetry Multiprocessor Architecture Overview,* 1991.

5. Intel Corporation, *Parallel Processing on Intel Hypercube Systems: A Technical Seminar,* (1991).

6. R. Mehrotra and E. F. Gehringer, "Superlinear Speedup Through Randomized Algorithms," *Proceedings of the 1985 International Conference on Parallel Processing,* August 1985, pp. 291–300.

7. Intel Corporation, *iPSC/860 Specifications,* (1991).

8. J. Van Zandt, "C3I Beyond the von Neumann Bottleneck," *Defense Electronics,* January 1986.

3

Early Generations of Parallel Processors

"Begin at the beginning," the King said, very gravely, "and go on till you come to the end: then stop."
Lewis Carroll, *Alice's Adventures in Wonderland*

Even in the early days of computing, engineers were designing and building computers with multiple processors. The design objective for these early machines was not usually performance on a single application. The focus was usually on reliability or on throughput for a number of tasks. A few of the first multiprocessors are shown in Figure 3-1.

Computer	Company	Processors	Introduced
D-825	Burroughs Corporation	4 processors 16 I/O processors	1962
B5500	Burroughs Corporation	2 processors	1963
System 360/67	IBM	3 processors	1967

Figure 3-1. *Early multiprocessor computers*

One of the first such machines was the D-825.[1] The D-825, designed by Burroughs Corporation in 1962, had up to four processors. The primary purpose of this parallel processor was not performance or throughput, but availability. That is, the machine was designed in a modular fashion so that in the event of an error, the machine could still be used. It was not until the early 1970s that serious efforts to build high-performance computers out of multiple processors began.

First Generation

The first generation of true parallel processors (machines in which multiple processors are used to improve performance in executing a single application) was designed in experimental computer science departments and research labs. Two of the most complete systems, with significant software as well as hardware components, were the Illiac IV[2] (designed at the University of Illinois at Urbana-Champaign) and the C.mmp[3] (designed at Carnegie-Mellon University). Many other research prototypes were developed only on paper or with a lesser level of hardware and software. The Illiac IV and the C.mmp are chosen here because they best represent the two classes of parallel processors: SIMD and MIMD, respectively. Both were in production use for many years. The Illiac IV was used for numerical computations, such as synthetic-aperture radar, weather modeling, and space shuttle reentry simulation,[4] from the mid-1970s through the early 1980s, when it was replaced by a Cray-1. The C.mmp was used from mid-1975 through the mid-1980s as a general time-sharing computer for the computer science department at Carnegie-Mellon University.

The Illiac IV

The Illiac IV project began in the late 1960s at the University of Illinois, with a goal of achieving one billion instructions per second (1000 MIPS). The idea was to design a computer with 256 processing elements, each of which could execute 4 million instructions per second. The design called for the processing elements to be grouped in quadrants, with 64 processing elements per quadrant.

Because of technology and funding problems encountered during the project, only one quadrant was actually built. It achieved approximately 200 million instructions per second.

The Illiac IV, shown in Figure 3-2, can be classified as a SIMD computer. Each of the processing elements (PE) executes instructions, which are given by the central control unit (CU), if the PE is in active mode. Certain instructions can cause individual PEs to go either active or inactive, based on the results of a calculation. This is standard in SIMD machines today: Each PE has its own private memory for storing data; there is no global shared memory.

The PEs were interconnected using a nearest-neighbor interconnection scheme (shown in Figure 3-3). This meant that if a piece of data was needed by a PE at the other side of the network, many instruction steps were required to move the data from one PE to another until it arrived at the appropriate destination. This inability to randomly send data from one PE to another turned out to be a significant limiter on the computer's use for a wide class of applications. As we shall see, this limitation has been removed for most third-generation parallel processors.

Figure 3-4 shows the Kiviat diagram for the Illiac IV. A *Kiviat diagram* is a graphical method for displaying multiple metrics of goodness of a computer architecture. Circular graphs for showing

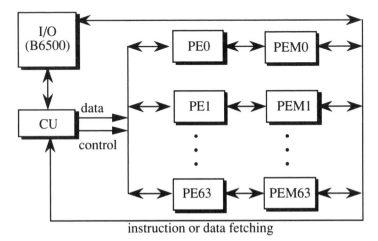

instruction or data fetching

Figure 3-2. *The Illiac IV*

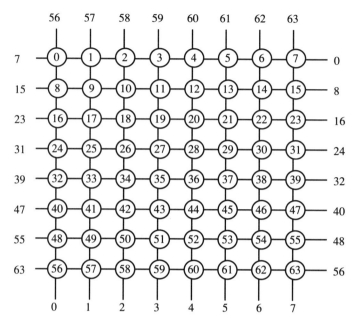

Figure 3-3. *Illiac IV processing element interconnection scheme*

computer performance were first used by Kolence,[5] who named them after Philip Kiviat (then Technical Director at Fedsim in Washington, D.C.) who, he said, first suggested the idea. A Kiviat diagram's value is that it presents a very visual way to compare computer architectures, which take advantage of human pattern recognition capabilities.

In Figure 3-4, the three characteristic "metrics" are the processor performance in MIPS, the memory size in megabytes, and the I/O bandwidth in megabits per second. These three metrics are chosen because of work done by Gene Amdahl, one of the computer architects of the IBM 360, who showed that the performance of a machine (in terms of instructions per second) is related to its amount of memory and I/O bandwidth. Amdahl postulated that a balanced general-purpose computer needed one megabyte of main memory for every million instructions per second (MIPS) that it could execute, and that such a machine also needed one megabit per second of I/O bandwidth (disk) for every MIPS. If these ratios hold, then the computer is balanced. If a machine violates these, then the added performance along one of

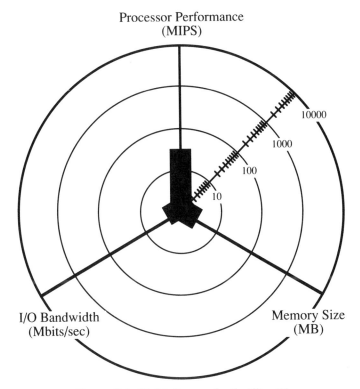

Figure 3-4. *Kiviat diagram for the Illiac IV*

the metrics does not translate into improved overall performance of the computer. These are known as Amdahl's Laws.

Therefore, a perfectly balanced computer would have a Kiviat diagram with equal-sized bars for the processor performance, the memory size, and the I/O bandwidth.

Now, let's look at the Kiviat for the Illiac IV. Clearly, the processor performance is very unbalanced in relation to the I/O bandwidth and the memory size.

All of the I/O for the Illiac IV was carried out by a second computer, a B6500. It had card readers and punches, disks, and tape drives. This turned out to be a bottleneck for applications with large amounts of data. The bandwidth between the memories and the I/O meant that only problems with a significant amount of computation between I/O operations ran efficiently.

Nor was the size of the local memories (2048 64-bit words) sufficient to keep up with the processing power of the PEs. This limited the machine's applicability for a wide class of problems.

All of this showed in the performance numbers. The Illiac IV, with 64 processors, was rated at 15 million floating-point operations per second (MFLOPS). This was only three times as fast as the CDC 7600 (of the same era), which had only one processor. The Cray-1 was rated at 138 MFLOPS. Thus, even with 64 processors, the Illiac IV was not able to beat the conventional supercomputers and make the added investment in rewriting the program for parallelization worthwhile.

The C.mmp

The C.mmp is a classic example of the shared-memory MIMD classification discussed in the previous chapter. The design used minicomputers (off-the-shelf PDP-20s and PDP-40s) as the processors, and a crossbar switch (the "S" in Figure 3-5) that allowed

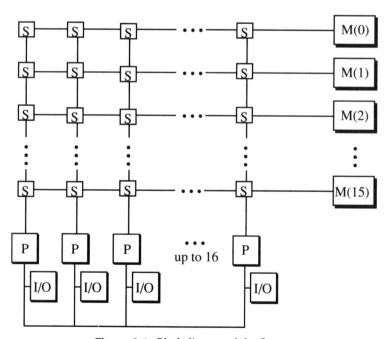

Figure 3-5. *Block diagram of the C.mmp*

any of the processors to access any word in the memory. In accordance with Amdahl's Law, the total memory for the system and the total I/O bandwidth scaled as the number of processors grew from 1 to 16. This can be seen in the Kiviat diagram for the C.mmp, shown in Figure 3-6.

The C.mmp project provided several lessons about parallel processors that helped guide later generations of computers.

The first and probably the most important lesson was about the performance. It was clearly demonstrated by a large number of applications that the performance of the C.mmp equaled or was better than state-of-the-art mainframes of that era. This meant that a large collection of relatively small and inexpensive processors could be linked together to create a computer with the performance of a large computer.

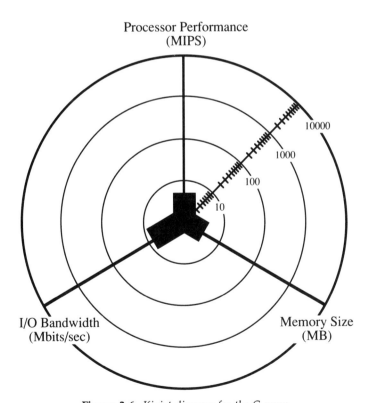

Figure 3-6. *Kiviat diagram for the C.mmp*

The second lesson was on reliability. Because parallel-processor computers are constructed out of many processors, the reliability of the whole is going to be worse than the reliability of a single processor. The C.mmp project showed that while the reliability of a single minicomputer was quite acceptable, the reliability of 16 minicomputers together was another matter.

This reliability problem was not intrinsic to parallel processors but a factor of the state of the technology in the 1970s. The problem went away with the advent of the microprocessor, because the reliability of microprocessors is far greater than that of high-performance processors built out of discrete components (such as minicomputers and mainframes). This is because reliability is inversely proportional to the number of components in a system, and a parallel processor constructed out of microprocessors has fewer components than a high-performance single-processor machine.

The third lesson was in the way the parallel processor interfaced to the world. Most parallel processors have been built as attached processors; that is, they are not capable of executing the whole application. Attached processors are used to execute the compute-intensive part of an application while the input and output, data storage, and user interface are all handled by a general-purpose computer. The C.mmp was not an attached processor; it was a general-purpose, stand-alone computer. All of the I/O devices were attached to it. It had an operating system that managed its resources in a time-sharing fashion. This is important, because very few problems are so computationally intensive that they require little I/O. Problems that require substantial I/O as part of the computation end up being I/O–bound, because the host computer's I/O subsystem cannot keep up with the attached processor.

Although the C.mmp did not attain supercomputer performance, it was still a successful experimental machine. It laid the groundwork for many of the general-purpose parallel processors that were to come.

Second Generation

Even though the members of the first generation were destined to be research machines that generated mainly academic interest, several pioneers foresaw the commercial potential of these machines. They recognized that the era of the monolithic supercomputer was nearing an end. Also, the Defense Advanced Research Projects Agency[6] (DARPA) was starting to take an active role in the advancement of the computer industry, specifically to enhance the national security of the United States. The Agency believed that computers would be a dominant part of all defensive systems from intelligence gathering to command and control. DARPA also foresaw that by helping to build a strong computing industry, the economic security of the nation would be enhanced. This philosophy, combined with an active venture-capital community, meshed to create many companies, whose products were to be the second generation of parallel processors and the first generation of commercial parallel computers. Figure 3-7 lists some of these machines.

However, these computers suffered from the same problems that the earlier machines did: the absence of true supercomputer performance, the difficulty of programming the parallelism, and the lack of substantial I/O.

Most of these second-generation parallel processors violated Amdahl's Laws, as will be shown, and in doing so they were relegated to be, for the most part, research curiosities, not to be taken seriously by the commercial world. It was not until the third generation that these obstacles were overcome.

Few of these machines, which seemed to spring to life simultaneously between 1983 and 1986, have survived. Many have lived only short lives, leaving their carcasses in laboratories around the world. We will discuss the survivors—whose descendants are still having a major impact in the parallel-processing arena.

BBN Butterfly

The first commercial parallel processor of the second generation was the BBN Butterfly, which was first used in 1981. It is classified as a MIMD computer. It is a cross between a shared-memory system and a distributed-memory system. As shown in Figure 3-8, each processor has its own local memory, but each processor also has the capability of directly addressing the memory of other processors. The advantage of this is that each processor

Company	Product	Classification	Number of processors
Alliant	FX/Series	MIMD (dist. mem.)	8
Ametek	Ametek 2000	MIMD (dist. mem.)	256
BBN	Butterfly	MIMD (shared mem.)	256
ELXSI	System 6400	MIMD (shared mem.)	12
Flexible Computer	Flex/32	MIMD (dist. mem.)	20
Floating Point	T Series	MIMD (dist. mem.)	16384
Goodyear	PEPE	SIMD	8
Goodyear	STARAN	SIMD	256
Goodyear	MPP	SIMD	65536
ICL	DAP	SIMD	4096
Intel	iPSC/1	MIMD (dist. mem.)	128
Loral	LDF 100	MIMD (dataflow)	256
Meiko	Computing Surface	MIMD (dist. mem.)	156
nCUBE	nCUBE/10	MIMD (dist. mem.)	1024
Sequent	Balance 21000	MIMD (shared mem.)	30
Thinking Machines	CM-1	SIMD	65536

Figure 3-7. *Second-generation parallel processors*

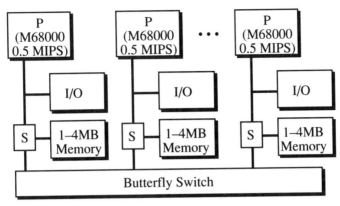

Figure 3-8. *The BBN Butterfly*

can access some amount of memory quickly, giving it better performance, while not giving up the benefit of a shared-memory programming model.

Each of the processors in the Butterfly[7] is a M68000, essentially a 0.5-MIPS processor. Since a Butterfly can have up to 256 processors, this gives it a peak performance of 128 MIPS. Each processor can also have an I/O bus. Each processor has 1 to 4 megabytes, yielding a total memory of 256 to 1024 MB for a 256-processor system. As can be seen in the Kiviat diagram in Figure 3-9, the system is surprisingly well-balanced by Amdahl's Laws.

The Butterfly missed commercial success partly because of its performance. The memory system design introduced a strong bias toward programs whose data could be partitioned into 1- to 4-MB chunks, so that each processor could have all of its data local. There was a large performance hit when one processor had to access another processor's memory; the access time to another processor's memory was 5 to 10 times slower than access to its local memory. This contributed to a peak performance well under that of contemporary supercomputers, against which it was targeted.

While the host computer for the Butterfly could run a standard operating system, the parallel processor used an operating system that was unique, so that applications had to be specially written for the Butterfly. This consigned the Butterfly to the re-

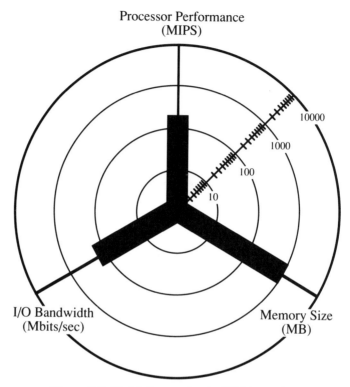

Figure 3-9. *Kiviat diagram for the BBN Butterfly*

search laboratories, where it was shown that near-linear speedup could be achieved on a variety of applications. However, without an effective operating system for managing and conventionally accessing data files, the system could not be used for many production environments.

TMC Connection Machine

The CM-1 is patterned after the Connection Machine,[8] which was an academic design and part of a doctoral dissertation. It was the first SIMD parallel processor to receive any sort of commercial success.

As with all SIMD computers to date, the computer trades off individual processor performance for number of processors. In the case of the CM-1, each processor operates on a single bit of data at a time (compared to most computers of the late 1980s, which operate on 32 to 64 bits at a time). The execution rate is only 4 MIPS (for 1-bit operations), compared to over 160 MIPS for the Cray X-MP. However, the CM-1 has 65,536 processors (see Figure 3-10), so the combined effect of executing all processors in parallel can yield performances almost—but not quite—in the supercomputer range.

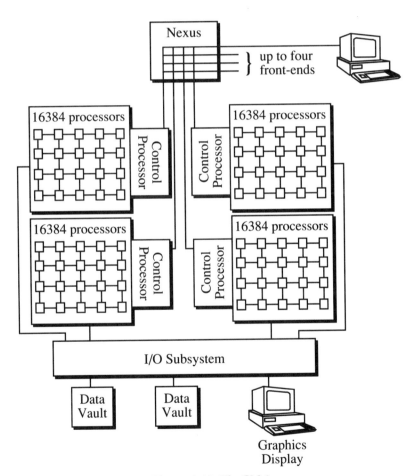

Figure 3-10. *The CM-1*

The processors execute instructions in a SIMD manner. A single instruction stream is generated by the control processor (sometimes referred to as the *front end*). Each processor has its own dataset. Each processor receives an instruction, for example ADD, and then performs the ADD operation on a local data item. In order to allow for conditional execution—processing which is dependent on the data—most of the instructions are conditional. That is, each processor has a flag that can be set dependent on the outcome of an instruction. If the flag is set, a conditional instruction is executed. If the flag is not set, the processor does not execute the instruction; instead, it waits until an unconditional instruction is sent from the control processor, or until it receives an instruction to set the flag.

With this processing style, it should be no surprise that problems that involve arrays of data (so that each processor has a part of the data) are very effective. These are problems like weather simulation, solving large matrices, and searching for information in a database. The third problem area actually exposes one of the main flaws of the CM-1. Most problems that require large amounts of processing power also require large amounts of data. Although the CM-1 is good at processing information that can be held in each processor's local memory, the performance of the machine can fall off precipitously if the data is larger than the local memories will hold.

The key feature that the CM-1 brought to the design of SIMD parallel processors is *pointer-based communication.*[9] Previous SIMD computers could transfer information only between processors that were nearest neighbors. This put a huge constraint on the class of applications that could efficiently run on the machines. With the pointer-based communication used in the CM-1, any processor can transfer a piece of data to any other processor with a single instruction. This broadens the class of applications on which the machine can perform well.

The Kiviat diagram for the CM-1 in Figure 3-11 shows that the computer was out of balance. Amdahl's law on the amount of memory the CM-1 should have can be calculated by assuming that each processor is really a 0.125-MIPS processor. To compare a one-bit processor with a more traditional word-oriented processor (say 32 bits per word), the performance of the CM-1 processor

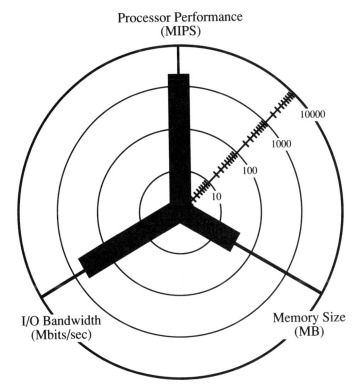

Figure 3-11. *Kiviat diagram for the CM-1*

is divided by 32 (4 MIPS/32 = 0.125 MIPS). Amdahl's law states that such a processor should have 128KB of memory. But in the CM-1 each processor has only 4K bits. This means that the total memory for the 65,536-processor CM-1 is only 32MB. Yet the performance of the combined processors is close to 8192 MIPS (peak performance). This imbalance greatly diminishes the machine's potential for real applications.

The I/O is out of balance, but not by as much. Amdahl's law would expect the CM-1 to have an I/O bandwidth of 1024 MB/second. The actual I/O bus for the CM-1 is about 512 MB/second, although the I/O subsystem cannot deliver that amount.

One other interesting point about the CM-1 and the other SIMD machines of this era is that they are all based around proprietary processors. While the other parallel processors are based around microprocessors (such as those that power PCs), the SIMD nature of the CM-1 requires a specially designed processor. In the long run, this may cause problems with SIMD machines in general, since the investment to design and maintain a proprietary processor (including the unique software) increases over time. Commodity microprocessors can amortize the investment over tens of millions of processors, whereas a CM-1 processor amortizes over tens of thousands. By itself, this economic argument might foretell the disappearance of SIMD machines.

Intel Scientific iPSC/1

Billed as a personal supercomputer, the iPSC/1[10] never quite lived up to its name. The performance of the machine, even with 128 processors, did not achieve supercomputer status. It took three generations of this class of machine to become competitive with supercomputers. What the iPSC/1 did was to lay the groundwork, showing that scientific programs could take advantage of the multiplicity of processors. Many research laboratories around the country bought small iPSC/1s, with only 8 to 16 processors, for experimentation.

As shown in Figure 3-12, this machine is a distributed-memory MIMD computer, also known as a multi-computer. It is a refinement of the design of the Cosmic Cube,[11] which was conceived and built at Caltech. Although the original machine at Caltech was built using the Intel 8086 microprocessor (yes, the chip that was in the first IBM PCs), the iPSC/1 used the Intel 80286, a later-generation processor with a performance of around 1 MIPS.

The iPSC/1 is often referred to as a *hypercube*, or just *cube*. This is because the original interconnection network that was used to connect the processors was a hypercube (see Chapter 2). Like the CM-1, this machine allowed messages (data) to be exchanged between any two processors in the system. This advantage over earlier parallel processors led to its use for a wider range of applications.

The iPSC/1 is not a stand-alone computer but is attached to a host (the Cube Manager in Figure 3-12) that is responsible for

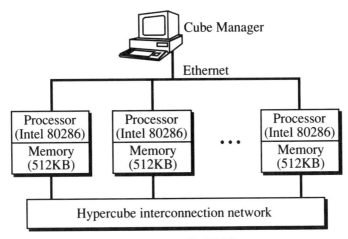

Figure 3-12. *The iPSC/1*

all the program development, the loading, and the I/O. The host for the iPSC/1 is a PC, based on the Intel 80286 microprocessor. The original concept was that some applications require very little I/O and are exceptionally compute-intensive. For these applications, the user would program the parallel processors, load a small amount of data into the memories of the processors, and then let the machine crunch the data for several minutes to several hours. This is very similar to the CM-1, just described. This also violates the I/O portion of Amdahl's Laws, as can be seen in the Kiviat diagram in Figure 3-13. What users of the iPSC/1 soon discovered was that although the parallel processors could execute the computational portion of the problem, few real problems were that constrained.

The machine was designed for a single user. (This was later changed to allow users to partition the machine into fixed-size sections.) To program it, the user writes a program for each node in the system. Usually, the same program can be used for all processors. Embedded in the program are explicit statements to send and receive messages (data) with other processors in the system.

Communication between the host and the processors is also done via messages. To perform I/O (a disk operation), a message

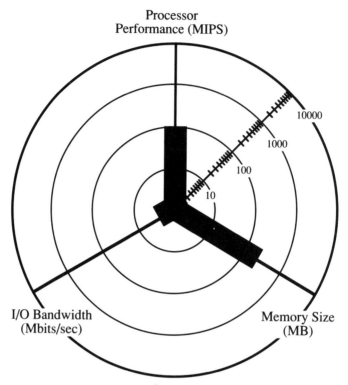

Figure 3-13. *Kiviat diagram for the iPSC/1*

is sent to the host, and the host performs the read operation and sends a message, containing the results of the disk read operation, back to the processor. Note that this is a great bottleneck if more than a few processors request data simultaneously.

Sequent Balance

The Balance family of computers was the first of a line of parallel processors that would become one of the most successful in the parallel processing arena. By the end of 1990, there had been over 3000 Sequent parallel processors installed worldwide.

The Balance[12] architecture can be classified as a shared-memory MIMD parallel processor. This means that the (up to 30) processors all share the main memory. The standard problem with a shared-memory machine is in the performance degradation that can occur as more processors try to access the shared memory. The memory (and the bus) can become a bottleneck to scalability.

The Balance designers developed a unique twist to this architecture, avoiding the performance degradation problem and delivering a machine that scales almost linearly up to 30 processors. This architectural twist gives each processor a cache memory (see Figure 3-14). The processors have the advantage of using the cache as a local memory that can be accessed quickly for performance, without losing the significant advantage of a shared-memory programming model.

A cache memory is a high-speed memory that is local to a processor. Its purpose is to hold frequently used blocks of main memory. The concept behind cache memory is that a typical program does not access all parts of memory evenly. Also, once a program accesses a particular address in memory, there is a high likelihood that the same address (or one nearby) will be accessed in the near future. The management of the cache is handled completely by hardware, so the programmer is unaware of its existence.

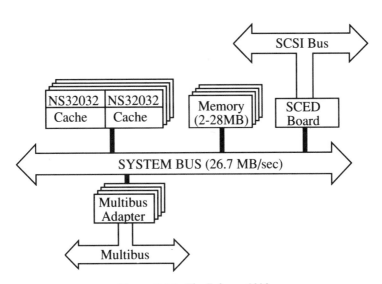

Figure 3-14. *The Balance 8000*

Caches are found in high-performance single-processor computers as well as in some multiprocessors today, but in 1985 this was unique among parallel processors. Multiprocessor caches add a level of complexity to the cache design. Since each cache contains a copy of data that is in memory, it is important that all processors in a system stay *coherent;* that is, that all processors see the same value in a particular memory location, regardless of which cache the actual data is in, or which processor most recently changed the data.

The Balance computer was designed to allow users the benefits of parallel processing in two ways: through standard multiprocessing and through parallel processing.

The multiprocessing features of Balance are highlighted by recognizing that the UNIX operating system already contains multiprocessing primitives that programs use to advantage on single-processor computers. Since the Balance operating system was derived from UNIX, any program that runs on UNIX can be recompiled for the Balance and run. But instead of being time-shared on a single processor, the program has access to the multiple processors. Thus, multiprocessing programs get the immediate benefit of parallel processors.

The second approach is the use of shared memory and primitives that allow programs to be rewritten to take advantage of the parallel processors. This approach is similar to the approaches of other parallel processors. The big advantages of the Sequent Balance are that the parallel program can run simultaneously with more standard multiprocessing programs, and that it can have the complete benefit of UNIX and applications that run under UNIX.

The machine is very balanced in terms of Amdahl's Laws, as shown by Figure 3-15. With 30 processors, the machine could deliver 21 MIPS. This doesn't seem like a lot of performance by today's standards, but in 1985 a typical mainframe delivered only 10 to 15 MIPS. The main memory could be expanded to 28 MB.

The I/O subsystem is comprised of disk controllers and Multibus interfaces. The bandwidth from these is over 10 MB per second, with the limit being the system bus at 26.7 MB per second. This is much more than the 4 MB per second that Amdahl's Laws suggest is necessary.

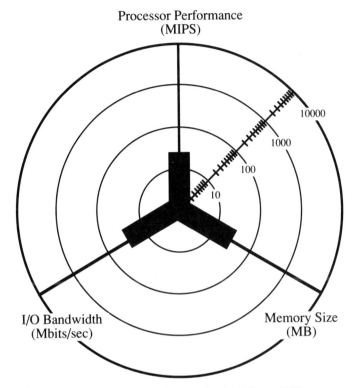

Figure 3-15. *Kiviat diagram for the Balance 8000*

This is one of the first parallel processors that experienced success in the commercial marketplace; its successor Sequent computers would vastly outsell their competitors. In particular, their success was in the information systems arena, especially in relational databases (RDBMS), because of:

- Multiprocessing features that allowed RDBMS's (which already took advantage of multiprocessing) to utilize the parallel processors and show a performance gain without any reprogramming.
- The integrated I/O system, which offered full functionality of UNIX directly from the parallel processors and was balanced with respect to performance.
- Incremental performance improvements to applications, which could be achieved by tuning them to the parallel processors.

Summary

The first generation of parallel processors faced several obstacles. The primary obstacles were the inability to deliver performance and the necessity for programming that was totally different from the type required for sequential processors. "Dusty-deck" programs would not run fast on these machines. The top-of-the-line supercomputers (the Crays and the CDC machines) were still several orders of magnitude faster than these parallel machines. The price/performance of the machines, though significantly better than the supercomputers, did not make up for it. If the user had enough money to buy any computer in the world and speed was the primary motivator (such as for "big science" problems or government agencies), then price was no object and the supercomputers won. If the user was on a limited budget but performance was critical, the user would use Cray time to avoid paying for the reprogramming of large applications for the parallel processor.

Also fundamental to the lack of first-generation commercial success was the absence of I/O capability. As long as the problem required little input or interaction with existing information systems, and generated little output, these machines were very good. But they were not capable of I/O rates comparable to those of traditional computers. Amdahl's Laws state that a machine needs a certain amount of I/O bandwidth and memory size to be effective. The second generation of parallel processors ignored this fundamental constraint and created machines that were mostly used only for research on how to parallelize applications.

Secondary issues were the stability of the hardware, the total lack of good software for development and execution, and the skepticism of the user base. For the most part, these machines were relegated to the research labs and universities experimenting with parallel processing. As late as 1988, many companies were just starting to investigate whether parallel processing would help them solve their problems more cost-effectively.

Key Points

1. The second generation of parallel processors showed that a wide collection of applications could be parallelized and efficiently executed.

2. Amdahl's Laws apply to parallel processors, in that computers must be balanced in the amount of main memory and the amount of I/O they support in relation to their performance.

3. By the mid-1980s some parallel processors were just beginning to show that they could effectively attack commercial information system problems.

References

1. J. P. Anderson, S. A. Hoffman, J. Shifman, and R. J. Williams, "D825—A Multiple Computer System for Command and Control," *Proceedings of the FJCC*, vol. 22, 1962, pp. 86–96.

2. W. J. Bouknight, S. A. Denenberg, D. E. McIntyre, J. M. Randall, A. H. Sameh, D. L. Slotnick, "The Illiac IV System," *Proceedings of the IEEE*, April 1972, pp. 369–388.

3. H. H. Mashburn, "The C.mmp/Hydra Project: An Architectural Overview," *Computer Structures: Principles and Examples*, in D. Siewiorek, G. Bell, A. Newell, eds. McGraw-Hill, New York, N.Y., 1982.

4. G. Feierbach, and D. Stevenson, "The Illiac IV," in *Infotech State of the Art Report on Supercomputers*, Maidenhead, England, 1979.

5. K. Kolence, *Performance Evaluation Review*, June 1973.

6. Defense Advanced Research Projects Agency, *Strategic Computing*, October 1983.

7. BBN Laboratories, *Butterfly Parallel Processor Overview*, June 1986.

8. W. D. Hillis, *The Connection Machine*, (Cambridge, MA: MIT Press), 1985.

9. W. D. Hillis, G. L. Steele, Jr., "Data Parallel Algorithms," *Communications of the ACM*, vol. 29, December 1986, pp. 1170–1183.

10. J. Rattner, "Concurrent Processing: A New Direction in Scientific Computing," *AFIPS Conference Proceedings*, vol. 54, 1985.

11. C. Seitz, "The Cosmic Cube," *Communications of the ACM*, January 1985, pp. 22–33.

12. Sequent Computer Systems, Inc., *Balance 8000 System Technical Summary*, 1985.

4

The Third Generation—
Commercializing
Parallel Processing

When you were a tadpole and I was a fish,
In the Paleozoic time,
And side by side on the ebbing tide,
We sprawled through the ooze and slime.
                    Langdon Smith, *Evolution*

Having covered the history and evolution of parallel processors in the previous chapters, we will now describe in detail four premier computers that represent the state of the art in parallel processors.

Reasons for Success

The current generation of parallel processors, the third generation, has finally started showing up en masse in commercial environments, solving real problems and affecting financial bottom lines. Companies are finding that machine performance, as well as attractive price/performance, are enabling problem solving that could not be done before, in a timeframe that can provide immediate results. Companies no longer have to wait for inventory reports and financial analyses. In an era in which information is power, parallel processors are putting power into the hands of company executives. There are three primary reasons for the success:

- The third generation of parallel processors is achieving mainframe and supercomputer levels of performance that justify investment in programming.
- This generation of parallel processors focuses more on the complete system, thereby balancing the system to match the processing power.
- Several parallel processors have refined an approach that enables the immediate use of large numbers of applications.

We are going to look at four computers that are truly breaking down the doors and establishing themselves in the commercial marketplace. Each is doing it in a different way, and each has had differing levels of success. The Sequent Symmetry 2000 series has been successful as an information systems platform for relational database-based applications. The MasPar MP-1, a new generation of SIMD machines targeted at the simulation and numeric computation market, incorporates many new approaches to this form of parallel processing. The Intel iPSC/860 is included because of its success in delivering supercomputer performance for a wide range of scientific applications. Finally, the Teradata DBC/1012 computer is a specialized parallel processor focused on the database server market, with many customers in the *Fortune* 200.

Sequent Symmetry 2000

Sequent Computer Systems (Figure 4-1) has been producing parallel processors for over eight years. Sequent is one of the most successful of the parallel-processing computer companies, having shipped over 4000 parallel processors. The Sequent Symmetry 2000[1] is the latest in its line of computer systems.

Product Line Description

Of the parallel processors, the Sequent machines are probably the most oriented toward the general-purpose commercial informa-

Company	Sequent Computer Systems, Inc. 15450 SW Koll Parkway Beaverton, OR 97006
Contact	Rick Gimbel Manager, Marketing Communication (503) 578-5700
Number of Employees	approx. 1400
Revenue (1991)	$213M
Product(s)	Symmetry 2000/40, 2000/200, 2000/400, 2000/700
Installed base (1991)	approx. 4000

Figure 4-1. *Sequent Computer Systems background*

tion systems (IS) environment. Since Sequent offers the same operating system and applications for the entire range of platforms, the product line provides complete compatibility from a one-processor system (Sequent Symmetry 2000/40) to a 30-processor Symmetry 2000/700. Performance ranges from desktop to mainframe.

The entire product is based on open systems standards, which allow applications to be portable across computers and operating systems. Open systems are important because they protect the customer's major investment—application development, maintenance, and training—while freeing the customer from complete dependence on a single computer manufacturer. The networking connections are based on the X/Open standards. The operating system is based on UNIX.

History

The Balance 8000 and the Balance 21000 were the first two computers that Sequent shipped, starting in 1985. (These are described in more detail in Chapter 3.) The Balance computers were second-generation parallel processors, shared-memory MIMD computers that ran a multiprocessing version of UNIX. Balance computers are still operating in computer centers today. Sequent coined the term *symmetric multiprocessing* to describe their brand of parallelism. It is no different than shared-memory MIMD computers as described in Chapter 2.

The Symmetry line of computers, also shared-memory MIMD machines, were first shipped in 1987. One of the most important characteristics of the Symmetry line has been its ability to protect customers' investments by allowing system upgrades as technology has improved. For example, over the lifetime of the Symmetry line, the microprocessors have changed four times, and customers could upgrade their processors without replacing the whole computer. This has provided an increase in performance of almost ten times over the past four years. This is in stark contrast to traditional computers, which require replacement of the old computer with a complete new computer in order to take advantage of the latest technology and performance.

Company

Today's parallel processors are not solely the domain of startups and small companies. Though Sequent was founded in 1983 by 17 people, the company has grown at an astounding rate; in 1991, revenues exceeded $213 million. The total installed base for the company, including the Balance and Symmetry product lines, is over 4000 computers, over 10 times more than any other parallel processor.

The company's headquarters and main R&D facility is in Beaverton, Oregon. The company offers worldwide sales and service. It established a second R&D center, in France, during 1991.

Classification and Block Diagram

The Symmetry line is composed of four separate models. Each model has certain limits on the number of slots into which boards can be placed, the style of I/O supported, and the performance of the bus (which places limits on the scalability of different models). At the bottom end, the Symmetry 2000/40 is fundamentally different from other models, in that it is designed to be a one-processor system with heavy levels of integration and packaging. However, it is software-compatible with all the other members of the family. At the top end is the Symmetry 2000/700, capable of supporting 30 processors, with disks and memory to match—an example of the scalability of this design. Scalability is one of the main reasons companies buy parallel processors. It allows them to start small and grow, or to have the same system in different sites tuned to different processing requirements. Figure 4-2 shows the performance of the Sequent Symmetry 2000 on the standard TPC-B database benchmark (Chapter 7). It shows that as the number of processors is increased, the performance scales linearly.

The central hardware feature of the Symmetry 2000/700 is the Symmetry Bus (Figure 4-3). This is how data is transferred among processors as well as between the processors and the I/O. Each processor has a cache, as in the Balance line (Chapter 3), which is used to hold instructions and data the processor has accessed recently or will be accessing in the near future. This drastically improves the performance of the machine, by allowing the processors to execute at their full potential without having to wait for memory accesses to travel from the processor to the memory system. If the caches were not there, system performance would not be nearly as good.

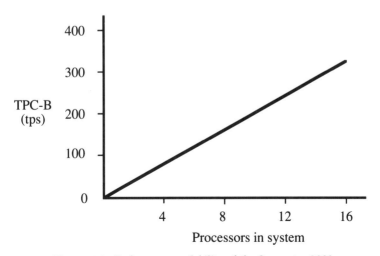

Figure 4-2. *Performance scalability of the Symmetry 2000*

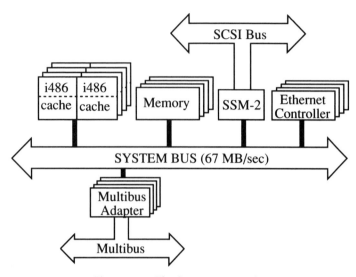

Figure 4-3. *The Symmetry 2000/700*

One of the difficult problems that the company solved, for both the Balance and Symmetry lines, was *cache coherency:* making sure that all processors always see the same data at the same memory location. In the Symmetry line, the algorithms that do this are buried in an application-specific integrated circuit (ASIC) for each processor. An ASIC is a custom-designed chip that provides needed performance and functionality.

Symmetry systems have used a wide range of microprocessors as the central processing elements. The current generation, the Symmetry 2000, uses Intel 486 microprocessors, which deliver 14 million instructions per second (MIPS) of performance per processor. Combined, the processing power of a 30-processor system exceeds 420 MIPS.

The Symmetry line can accommodate up to 816 megabytes (MB) of main memory. This amount varies based on the number of boards in the system (number of slots available) and the current level of memory chip technology.

The I/O is accomplished in several ways. Certain high-speed I/O controllers are attached directly to the Symmetry bus. These include the disk controllers, which support the high-speed disks, and the Ethernet controllers. Other controllers are attached via a

Multibus or a VME bus, standard buses for which a wide variety of third-party I/O devices are available. A special interface exists between these I/O buses and the Symmetry bus.

How Amdahl's Laws Are Addressed

Looking at the Symmetry 2000/700, we see that it can have up to 30 processors. The top end of the line uses 30 Intel 486 processors, which, at 25 MHz, yield 14 MIPS each. Amdahl's Laws state that such a machine, with a total capacity of 420 MIPS, should have a main memory of 420 megabytes. The actual amount of memory that can be configured in the system is 816 MB, thus satisfying the memory requirement. The I/O system can send a maximum of 67 MB per second of data, which is a little over 500 megabits per second. All of these numbers conform nicely to Amdahl's Laws. In fact, the system could take another generation of higher-performing processors and still be well balanced.

In analyzing the Symmetry system, we find that Amdahl's Laws are obeyed. The Kiviat diagram (Figure 4-4) shows that the system is balanced and should be capable of handling a wide variety of applications commensurate with the performance.

Connectivity

No computer is an island. To be effective, it must be able to work with other computers in a much larger network. This is especially true for the high-performance machines, which are usually adjuncts to an already established computing environment.

In the past, the performance of network connectivity was a function of the performance of a single processor. Sequent has developed a Parallel STREAMS[2] technology that enables the communications performance to scale with the number of processors. This leads to vastly improved communications I/O, which is balanced with the processor performance.

What Changed to Make It Successful

Whereas the early Sequent product line (the Balance series, described in Chapter 3) was mildly successful, the later Symmetry series definitely took hold in the commercial marketplace. The primary reasons were that the balanced processor, memory, and

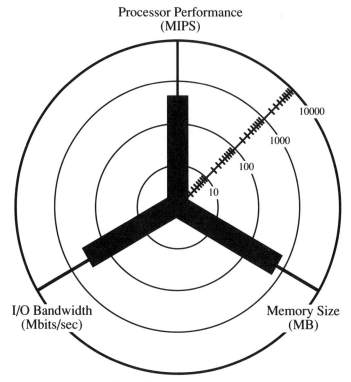

Figure 4-4. *Kiviat diagram for the Symmetry 2000/700*

I/O capability enabled the machine to execute relational databases very effectively and that acceptance of open systems as a computing base was growing.

Working with RDBMS
Most information systems applications are built on top of a database of one form or another. For a parallel processor to be successful in those applications, it either must be able to run the database management system (DBMS) directly or must be able to interact efficiently with a DBMS on a different computer. DBMS's historically are one of three types: *hierarchical, network,* or *relational.*

Hierarchical and network DBMS's, the original two forms, suffered from the inability to accommodate much change to their database structure. In commercial information systems, change is ever-present. Relational DBMS's (RDBMS) were originally defined in the early 1970s but were inefficient compared to hierarchical and network DBMS's. This meant that they were seldom used, even though they provided a substantial improvement in flexibility. As with most software technologies that improve programmer and user productivity, the tradeoff was to consume more computer power and less "consumer" power.

In the 1980s, the underlying software algorithms for RDBMS's improved efficiency to a level where they were starting to be used for new applications. Several companies developed their RDBMS software on top of the UNIX operating system. As part of the implementation, the RDBMS's used the multiprocessing primitives of UNIX. This turned out to be fortuitous for Sequent.

Sequent's brand of parallel processor was designed to use both conventional multiprocessing, as implemented in UNIX (although by using multiple processors rather than by time-sharing one processor), and conventional parallel processing (allowing a single task to utilize more than one processor). The result is that RDBMS's are easily ported to the Sequent parallel processor and naturally take advantage of the multiple processors with little modification.

This greatly enhanced performance for RDBMS's on mid-size computers. Combined with the robust I/O subsystem, it made the Sequent machine an attractive platform for the commercial information systems departments.

Acceptance of Open Systems
The Sequent Symmetry applied parallel processing to the standard multiprocessing of UNIX, and it had a balanced system. As UNIX became more popular with information systems departments, the Sequent machine became the leader in price/performance for mid-range platforms. Because open systems allowed applications to be independent of the underlying layers of software and hardware, users were not inextricably linked to any one vendor of platforms. The price/performance advantage and complete I/O functionality of the Sequent systems helped propel them into the IS market.

▼

DATABASE SERVER (SERVED THROUGH PARALLEL PROCESSING)

For seven years, Merrill Lynch & Co. had been paying $1 million per year in maintenance and leasing for an IBM mainframe. The system had been the center of the information system for the investment banking system. Then, in 1990, they gave the system back to IBM. What replaced it was a network of 1,100 personal computers and a parallel processor.

Over the years, the main applications that had run on the mainframe migrated to the personal computers. The result left the mainframe as little more than an information repository and server. It became clear to Joseph Freitas, the person whose vision helped rearchitect the information system at Merrill Lynch & Co., that the mainframe could be replaced by a computer designed more as a database server, and for a lot less money. For only $500,000, he was able to buy a Sequent Computer Systems' Symmetry parallel processor, which completely replaced the IBM mainframe.

With specialized software to manage the network and keep track of the location of the information among the PCs and the server, investment bankers at Merrill are today able to access and update client information instantly, a task which used to take days. Under the new system, a banker who visits a client enters in a report on his PC. It is then automatically routed to the central server and made available to any other computer in the network.

This new technology, Merrill believes, gives it an edge over the competition. As with many other businesses, faster, more up-to-date information serves the customers better. And parallel processors can lead the way. Of course, having the system be less expensive than the mainframe never hurts.

Source: Evan I. Schwartz, "The Dinosaur That Cost Merrill Lynch A Million A Year," *Business Week,* November 26, 1990.

Applications Well-Suited to This Machine

The Symmetry 2000 is oriented toward a general-purpose computing environment, and because the machine runs a version of UNIX, many applications are available off the shelf. Listed below are classes of applications that naturally take advantage of the Symmetry parallel processing system: client/server applications, text database applications, and object-oriented systems. In general, applications that are configured with many tasks and significant I/O requirements are ideal for this computer.

Client/Server Applications

In this approach, any application can be thought of as a service (the *server*) and a customer of that service (the *client*). Although the two parts may reside on the same computer, the program design philosophy makes building large, multiuser applications easier. For example, a DBMS can be thought of as a client/server architecture. The front end of the DBMS is actually a client that interfaces with the user (or program), takes the database query, and formulates the request to send to the database. The server is the back end of the DBMS, which takes the request and performs the requested operation(s).

Such applications are naturally expressed as a multiprocessing program. As such, they are perfect matches for parallel processors like the Sequent Symmetry, where the underlying system software enables the multiprocessing to take advantage of the parallel processors. This is clearly why RDBMS's are so successful on the Symmetry. The characteristics of client/server computing are heavy networking, multiprocessing with many simultaneous users, and, most often, databases. The I/O capacity of the Sequent machines, combined with their natural multiprocessing ability, makes them a good fit for client/server applications.

Text Databases

As more and more information is generated and disseminated electronically, volumincus quantities of text information are available. Somewhere within this text is information that can assist a company in being competitive. Imagine a company of 1000 people who communicate by electronic mail (email). Policy statements, company procedures, competitive information, design decisions, status information, and so on are all communicated in electronic text. In only a couple of years, this could add up to several gigabytes of information. If the information could be captured in an easily accessible online form, eliminating the effort of answering the same question multiple times would be a productivity gain and lead to a better competitive position. Being able to learn from past information about how to improve company processes and procedures could be a much bigger win.

Text database technology allows access to unstructured data, such as large quantities of text information, and enables searches of vast amounts of data in seconds. This problem is both processor- and I/O-intensive because of the dataset sizes involved. Parallel processors, especially ones like the Sequent Symmetry, are ideal for executing these applications.[3]

Object-Oriented Systems

Object-oriented programming is a new paradigm for writing software. In this paradigm, a program becomes a set of *objects*, which communicate by passing *messages* back and forth. An object is a collection of data elements as well as the code that defines the operations on the data.

Not only are there object-oriented programs, but there are also object-oriented database management systems. Object-oriented systems consume large amounts of memory, require significant task switching, and are usually implemented as multiprocessing systems. All of this points to the Symmetry style of parallel processing as an ideal platform for such systems.

MasPar MP-1

MasPar (Figure 4-5) is a relatively new company that, as its name implies, is devoted to bringing massively parallel computers to the commercial marketplace. *Massively parallel* is a nonscientific term that usually refers to computers with hundreds or thousands of processors. The MP-1, with up to 16,384 processors, is no doubt massively parallel.[4,5,6]

Company	MasPar Computer Corporation 749 North Mary Avenue Sunnyvale, California 94086
Contact	Ms. Kathy Lee Director, Marketing Communications (408) 736-3300
Number of Employees	130 (mid 1991)
Revenue	not publicly disclosed
Product(s)	MP-1 Data Parallel Computer 1100 with 1K–4K processors, 1200 Series with 1K–16K processors, options for 16KB or 64KB memory per processor (up to 1GB in system).
Installed base	60 revenue units in September 1991

Figure 4-5. *MasPar Computer Corporation background*

Product Line Description

The MP-1 is not a stand-alone computer but uses a front end processor for program development and as a control device for the I/O (although the I/O does not have to go through the front end). Unlike the CM-1 and CM-2 (Chapter 3), the MP-1's front end is very well integrated into the system, providing an almost seamless system.

The MP-1 comes in a variety of sizes. The basic processing unit is a board that contains 1024 processing elements. Up to 16 processor boards can be put into a system. The I/O subsystem is very robust and can use large disk arrays and high-speed graphics for visualization. The basic design allows the memory and communication bandwidths to scale as the number of processors is increased.

History

The MP-1 traces its history to machines like the CM-1, the MPP,[7] and the DEC MPP[8] (which was the actual predecessor to this machine). It is a classic SIMD machine, but with significant improvements over the second-generation SIMD machines, in particular in the I/O area and in the programming model. These will be described subsequently.

Company

MasPar was founded in 1988, and it shipped its first product in 1990. The company is still privately held, so there is no publicly available information about its finances. MasPar has recently announced an OEM relationship with DEC, which plans on marketing the MP-1.

Classification and Block Diagram

As we have seen in earlier chapters, one of the major failings of the early generations of parallel processors was their lack of sufficient I/O bandwidth to support the compute power. Also, the early parallel processor designers did not focus on the I/O problem; instead they concentrated on the processing unit. The MP-1 is very different from its predecessors in these regards. The block diagram in Figure 4-6 clearly demonstrates this: the I/O subsystem is well integrated into the overall computer.

The computer is composed of four major subsystems: the PE array, the UNIX subsystem, the I/O subsystem, and the interconnection network.

PE Array

The parallel processor portion of the MP-1 is in the processor element (PE) array. Each processor element is a 4-bit reduced-instruction-set computer (RISC), capable of executing just under two million 32-bit additions per second. Each processor element is simple, because there are very few control paths in its circuitry. The processors are small enough that 32 PEs fit on a single chip. Since this is a SIMD machine, all these chips take their instructions from the control unit. In the MP-1, this is called the Array Control Unit (ACU).

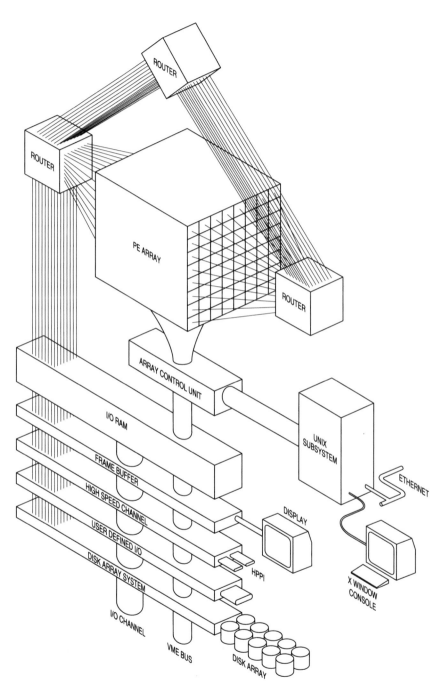

Figure 4-6. *Block diagram of the MP-1 (Courtesy of MasPar Computer Corporation.)*

The instructions for the processing elements are very similar to assembly language for any ordinary microprocessor. Each processing element has its own registers and can perform operations such as loading from memory, storing to memory, and adding two registers together. Unlike standard microprocessors, however, the processing elements have instructions that turn the processors on or off. These conditional instructions are at the heart of programming a SIMD machine, as we shall see in Chapter 6.

UNIX Subsystem

The UNIX subsystem provides standard operating system services to MP-1 programs and to the user. The development environment is hosted on this subsystem. System management is done through UNIX.

Whereas the I/O subsystem is designed for high-speed performance to match the processing power of the MP-1, all the low-speed peripherals and networks are attached to the UNIX subsystem. The processing elements must go through the UNIX subsystem for these low-speed I/O operations.

I/O Subsystem

The I/O subsystem and the processing elements are the heart of the MP-1. The I/O subsystem is designed to match data production and data consumption speeds between the PE array and high-speed I/O devices. As shown in Figure 4-6, the devices include disk arrays, a high-speed channel (HSC) interface, and a frame buffer for high-definition graphics, as well as a connection to allow user-defined I/O.

The I/O RAM, shown in Figure 4-6, is a buffer to hold I/O data that has been read or is to be written. This buffer holds up to 256 MB of memory.

Since the UNIX subsystem is responsible for all resource management functions, it is involved with I/O, but in an unobtrusive fashion. The UNIX subsystem opens and closes I/O devices. The Array Control Unit moves data into the I/O RAM at the speed of the interconnection network (which means it works at roughly the speed of the processing elements). Data transfer from the I/O RAM is under the control of either the UNIX subsystem or from the I/O processor for the device. In this way, data can move at speeds higher than the UNIX subsystem might be able to accommodate. This is a distinct advantage over earlier parallel processors like the BBN Butterfly or the iPSC/1, where the front end was involved in data transfers and was an I/O bottleneck.

Interconnection Network

The interconnection network for the MP-1 provides a high-speed path for data to be sent among processing elements and between processing elements and the I/O subsystem. As with the CM-1, the interconnection network allows random sending of data. That is, any processing element can send data to any destination with a single instruction. As was discussed with the CM-1 (in Chapter 3), this generalized capability was a major advancement over first-generation SIMD machines, in which the interconnection network imposed restrictions on where a processing element could send data.

How Amdahl's Laws Are Addressed

The Kiviat diagram for the MP-1 (Figure 4-7) shows a computer that strikes a different balance than that seen in other parallel processors. The I/O bandwidth, which historically has been the weakest link in a parallel processor (Chapter 3), is more closely matched to the processing performance than to the memory system. The memory system of the MP-1 is designed to allow an increase in total memory as the technology of memory chips improves, from 1-Mbit to 4- or 16-Mbit DRAM. This improvement will balance the memory and the I/O. This Kiviat diagram implies that the peak performance of the MP-1 (30,000 MIPS) will not be approached for the general class of problems. Instead, most applications will achieve a performance more balanced to the memory and the I/O, which will be in the 1000-MIPS range with the current generation of memory and in the 2000- to 5000-MIPS range with an improvement in the memory system.

Computationally intensive problems, which perform significant amounts of computation on each data element, are likely to achieve high percentages of peak performance. This class includes simulations involving three-dimensional models of real-world phenomena, data compression problems, and many three-dimensional matrix operations such as solving large systems of linear equations.

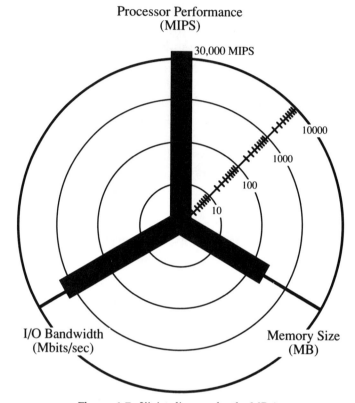

Figure 4-7. *Kiviat diagram for the MP-1*

The I/O capability of this machine is better than any other of the massively parallel computers, such as the iPSC/860 (described in the next section). Because of the separate I/O subsystem with the I/O RAM as a buffer, the MP-1 can drive high-performance networks, approaching 1 Gbit per second, or supercomputer interfaces like the HSC. This effectively allows it to perform the computation in parallel and yet execute the I/O in a conventional manner.

The other distinct advantage to the MasPar I/O subsystem is the benefit derived from the I/O RAM buffer. By its very nature, I/O does not lend itself directly to scalability. In other words, high-speed I/O is not easily composed of many low-speed components. What the I/O RAM provides is an excellent buffer that allows the computational part of the machine to be composed of thousands of small processors while letting the I/O be composed of a few high-performance channels. A good way to see this is to imagine that the buffer were not there. To write a block of data on a 100-MB-per-second-interface to a network would then require coordinating and multiplexing hundreds of the processors at a time, with some very complicated software. With the I/O RAM in place, the processors can simply write their data into the random access memory; then a conventional I/O controller for the 100-MB-per-second network can read the data from the memory. This is a significant advantage.

Programming Model
The MP-1 is a SIMD machine. To take advantage of the parallelism, the machine is programmed in the same way that all SIMD machines are: The program is decomposed in a *data-parallel* manner. That is, for a large data set where the same calculations are to be performed on all the data, a data-parallel approach gives each processing element a portion of the data, and then the elements all operate on their portions simultaneously. (See Chapter 6 for a detailed description of data parallelism.)

Because of the tight integration of the UNIX subsystem with the rest of the computer, the programmer can write one program for the whole collection (the UNIX subsystem, the ACU, and the PE array) and let the compiler manage the interactions. The programmer can also write two programs, one for the UNIX subsystem and one for the ACU and PE array combination, in which case the programmer must specify the interprocess communication. Regardless of the approach, all of the application development uses programming tools on the UNIX subsystem.

What Changed to Make It Successful

Even though MasPar is a new company, the MP-1 is the best representative of the third generation of SIMD parallel processors. The key factors contributing to its success are that it demonstrably achieves supercomputer performance on a set of applications;[9,10] and it effectively (and naturally) handles the programming of the parallelism with only slight modifications to standard languages.

Achieving Supercomputer Performance

One of the basic computational paradigms used throughout many areas of scientific modeling is *computational fluid dynamics*. It is used in everything from aircraft design (computing how air flows over a wing) to meteorology (predicting the weather) and from oceanography (modeling ocean currents) to geology (modeling oil field reservoirs).

Although the mathematics behind computational fluid dynamics are complex, the solution method is fairly straightforward. To model the airflow over a wing of an aircraft in flight, a basic data-parallel approach is taken. The wing is represented as a three-dimensional grid, with the nodes on the grid being the properties of the air near the wing. Since the same equations operate on each node of the grid to determine the change in properties of the air with each time step, the problem can be executed in parallel. Each processor in the MP-1 is given a set of the nodes from the grid. Then the machine just cycles through the equations. Figure 4-8 shows the results of different problem sizes (expressed as the number of points in each dimension). For large problems, the MP-1 is 25 percent faster than a Cray X-MP/132.[11]

Programming Ease

Even without using automatically parallelizing compilers (Chapter 6), standard languages such as C and Fortran, with minor extensions, have made the programming of MasPar machines relatively straightforward. Also, constructs are being added to the standard languages to allow the programmer to specify data

Problem Size	MasPar MP-1 Size	MP-1 Time (sec)	Cray X-MP/132 Time (sec)
30 x 25 x 30	1024	570	90
60 x 60 x 60	4096	1370	400
128 x 128 x 64	16384	1430	1800

Figure 4-8. *Performance of the MP-1 vs. a Cray X-MP/132*

parallelism (for example, Fortran 90). In addition, programmers have access to a robust set of tools for program construction, debugging, and machine animation. All of these tools are designed to take advantage of graphical X-based terminals, which helps programmers visualize programs and their parallelism.

Applications Well-Suited to This Machine

Applications that best use the MP-1's parallel processing performance are more computation-intensive than I/O-intensive. In fact, the ratio of computation to I/O for problems whose data set doesn't fit into memory is about 10:1, whereas for general applications it should be 1:1. It is also important to consider the number of floating-point operations when evaluating which applications are appropriate for the MP-1. Although this has nothing to do with the overall architecture of the machine, the processing element is not nearly as effective doing floating-point operations as it is doing integer arithmetic. The peak integer processing capability of the MP-1 is 30,000 MIPS; the peak floating-point performance is only 1500 MFLOPS.

Therefore, applications that fit the MP-1 tend to be numerical simulations of physical phenomena and scientific problems. And because of the well-integrated, high-performance I/O subsystem, it is also possible that some I/O-intensive applications might be a good fit for this machine.

Numerical Simulations of Physical Phenomena

These are problems in which discrete elements of an object (such as molecules, airplanes, cars, and people) are simulated. Each object usually has a number of different operations performed on it, making the computation-to-I/O ratio advantageous for the MP-1.

Although this approach to problem solving is currently more common in scientific disciplines than in business, it is likely to become part of decision support systems as they become better at modeling business operations in ever-increasing levels of detail.

These problems map well because, by their very nature, they have many elements that can be distributed among the processors. On the MP-1, each processing element usually gets a portion of the objects to be simulated. The program on the ACU then steps through the instructions, which causes the operations to be performed on the objects in parallel. The interconnection network, with its ability to exchange information between any two processors, allows objects to interact across processor boundaries.

Scientific Problems
Many applications in engineering and science require the solution of large systems of linear equations. The solution methodologies are often easily expressed as parallel algorithms.

Intel iPSC/860

The Intel iPSC/860 is a well-known parallel processor oriented toward the scientific marketplace. It is designed and built by the Supercomputer Systems Division of Intel Corporation (Figure 4-9).

Product Line Description

As the name of the division implies, the focus of the Intel product line has historically been to compete in the scientific supercomputer market. It wasn't until this generation that the iPSC/860 actually outperformed more traditional supercomputers, like the Cray-2, on real applications. The machine is not a stand-alone computer. It requires a host computer as its interface to the world. Program development, compilation, and loading of programs is done from the host (front-end) computer. The host is an i386-based PC. Mass storage is handled by disks, which either directly connect to the parallel processor or are attached (or accessed) through the host computer. Network connections to link the parallel processor with other computers are also done through the host.

History

The Intel iPSC/860 is the third in the line of parallel processors designed and built by Intel's Supercomputer Systems Division. The first generation, the iPSC/1, was described in Chapter 3.

Company	Intel Corporation, Supercomputer Systems Division 15201 NW Greenbrier Parkway Beaverton, OR 97006
Contact	Mike Bernhardt Marketing Relations (503) 629-7835
Number of Employees	not publicly disclosed
Revenue (1990)	Estimated at $29 million by Jeffrey Canin, a San Francisco–based industry consultant
Product(s)	iPSC/860, with 8, 16, 32, 64 or 128 nodes
Installed base (1991)	over 300

Figure 4-9. *Intel Supercomputer Systems Division background*

The second generation, the iPSC/2, improved on the interconnection network and changed from an Intel i286 to an Intel i386 processor. The iPSC/860's only improvement from the iPSC/2 is the upgrading of the microprocessor, which went from the i386 to an i860. All of the Intel parallel processors can be classified as distributed-memory MIMD machines. The first iPSC/860 machine was shipped in December of 1989. The three generations of Intel parallel processors have more than 300 machines in the field.

Company

The Intel Supercomputer Systems Division was founded in 1984 to develop a commercial version of the Cosmic Cube designed at Caltech. This is arguably the most successful of the supercomputer-oriented parallel processing companies, with a large installed base of over 300 machines.

Classification and Block Diagram

The iPSC/860 is a MIMD distributed-memory machine. The best way to think about the machine is as two distinct parts: the interconnection network and the nodes.

The interconnection network, which connects the processors (Intel calls them nodes), is used by the nodes to send messages to each other. Each message can be thought of as an envelope, marked with the address of the node the message is going to and a return address, and containing data. The node (or program) is responsible for putting the correct address on the message, and the network is totally responsible for delivering the message to the node with that address. How the network delivers the message is a matter of the hardware and is invisible to the programmer. For this reason, the actual structure of the network is irrelevant to the general functioning of the machine. However, if a programmer is trying to get the last ounce of performance out of the machine, intimate knowledge of the network structure and information about which processor is executing which part of the application are extremely important. Fine tuning such as this can improve performance by as much as 25 percent.

In the iPSC/860, there are two types of nodes: processing nodes and I/O nodes (see Figure 4-10). Processing nodes are based on the i860 microprocessor, which is oriented toward floating-point computations. I/O nodes are based on the i386 processor. Each I/O node has a SCSI interface to disk and tape.

To perform I/O, the processors send messages to the I/O nodes. The I/O nodes collect the messages and then perform the I/O. A critical difference between this and the MasPar MP-1 is the lack of something equivalent to the I/O RAM buffer of the MP-1. The performance of the I/O node is limited by the performance of the i386. More fundamentally, even with a faster processor for the I/O node there is no way to input or output a single high-performance stream of data, as required by certain types of imaging, scientific visualization, video, and gigabit networks. This is strictly due to the fact that the I/O must be sent to individual processors, with the resultant impedance mismatch.

Software

The programming environment provided by the iPSC/860 is hosted on the front-end computer, an i386-based PC. This com-

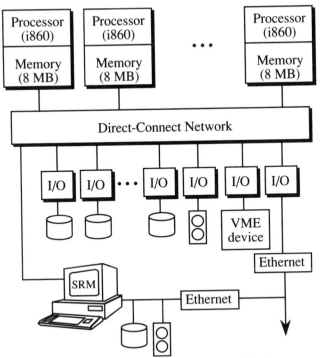

Figure 4-10. *Block diagram of the iPSC/860*

puter runs a version of the UNIX operating system and so provides all of the standard tools for developing programs. This is the computer that users interact with; there is no direct connection to the parallel processor.

Programmers write programs for the iPSC/860 in C or Fortran, inserting special library calls to carry out synchronization and communication between the parallel program parts. Programs are compiled on the host computer and then downloaded to the parallel processors. After this is accomplished, the programmer sends a message to the processors to start executing, which they do. Requests for operating services, such as I/O, special mathematical routines, and queries about system state, are all done via UNIX routine calls. The operating system for each of the processors simulates those interfaces or sends a request to the host computer to execute the routine, then passes the data back to the requesting processor.

Because of the special nature of the parallel processors, a user cannot run an existing application on the machine without modification. Since there are no multiprocessing primitives for the iPSC/860, programs that run as multiprocessing jobs under UNIX are not directly executable either.

How Amdahl's Laws Are Addressed

As can be seen by the Kiviat diagram for the iPSC/860 (Figure 4-11), processor performance is out of balance with the rest of the machine. Each processor node comes with only 1 MB of memory, even though the performance of each processor is rated at 40 MIPS and 40 MFLOPS. This means that applications with a high compute-to-data ratio will be able to take full advantage of this machine. However, more general-purpose applications will not

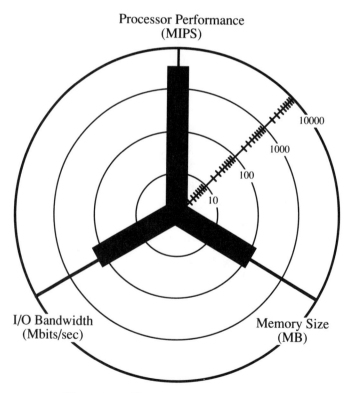

Figure 4-11. *Kiviat diagram for the iPSC/860*

perform up to the capabilities of the computer but will instead be limited by the bottlenecks of insufficient memory or insufficient I/O. For example, an application could quickly crunch through the data it has in memory, but it would then have to wait while the I/O system brought in more data to fill the memory.

In the iPSC/860, the actual limitation on how fast the memory can be filled is not the I/O nodes, but the interconnection network. Since the network has not been upgraded since the iPSC/2, iPSC/860 network performance is a maximum of 2.8 MB per second. Considering the overhead of the message-passing software, the actual rate at which data can be transferred between any two nodes in the system is a maximum of 2.6 MB per second. This seems like a lot until one looks at the performance of the processor. At 40 MIPS, the processor can perform 40 million additions in one second. This means that to keep busy with the data loaded into a node, the processor would have to perform 61 operations on each 4-byte number between I/Os.

Programming Model

The programming model is one of message passing between the nodes, using primitives provided in a library.

The typical approach is to write a single program, which is loaded onto all of the nodes. The program contains instructions that determine which node it is on and configures itself accordingly. For example, it might use its node number to determine which part of a matrix or file it should use as input and to compute which node should receive its results. Chapter 6 covers this in more detail.

What Changed to Make It Successful

Two things changed with the iPSC line of computers between the second and third generation to make them commercially successful: The third generation finally achieved the long-promised supercomputer performance, and it improved I/O to the point where larger, production-level problems could be tackled.

Achieving Better than Supercomputer Performance

The most compelling reason for the iPSC/860's success is its ability to outperform traditional supercomputers, like the Cray Y-MP and the Cray-2. And it does this at a price that is substantially less than the price of a supercomputer. For example, the top-of-the-line iPSC/860 is capable of performing 5.1 GFLOPS. (One GFLOPS is equal to 1000 MFLOPS, or 1 billion floating-point operations per second) and lists for $3.4 million.[12] A Cray Y-MP-8E, capable of executing only 2.8 GFLOPS (roughly half the performance of an iPSC/860), lists for over $15 million.[13] Even though the iPSC line offered a price/performance advantage, as long as its performance was lower than that of a supercomputer most users bought the supercomputer to avoid the cost of rewriting their programs. But now, those same users are turning toward the parallel processing of the iPSC/860, because the performance it offers gives them a competitive advantage.

▼

AND THE RACE GOES ON

As computer users have come to expect, the race for faster performance is ongoing. In June of 1991, Intel demonstrated a prototype computer, developed for DARPA at Caltech, with over 500 processors. The peak performance of this prototype was over 32 GFLOPS.

Developing Better I/O Capability

The other major change in the iPSC line is an improvement in I/O capability. The iPSC/860 has a Concurrent File System (CFS), which utilizes many disks in parallel to feed the processors. The interface to the file system is similar to the standard UNIX I/O. All parallel disk operation is hidden from the programmer. The CFS manages the placement and retrieval of data blocks from the multiple disks, which are spread across many I/O nodes.

Applications Well-Suited to This Machine

"Big" science and "grand challenges" (see the following box) are not the main consumers of supercomputing performance levels. Companies are finding that by applying the performance of supercomputers, they can stay ahead of the competition in key strategic areas. For example, they are designing products better and faster; they are detecting consumer buying trends; and they are tracking competitors more efficiently and completely by electronically searching through large amounts of information. Following are some of the areas where the iPSC/860 is being used most effectively.

"A *grand challenge* is a fundamental problem in science or engineering, with broad applications, whose solution would be enabled by the application of the high-performance computing that could become available in the near future. Examples of grand challenges are: (1) computational fluid dynamics for the design of hypersonic aircraft, efficient automobile bodies, and extremely quiet submarines, for weather forecasting for short and long term effects, efficient recovery of oil, and for many other applications; (2) electronic structure calculations for the design of new materials, such as chemical catalysts, immunological agents, and superconductors; (3) plasma dynamics for fusion energy technology and for safe and efficient military technology; (4) calculations to understand the fundamental nature of matter, including quantum chromodynamics and condensed matter theory; (5) symbolic computations including speech recognition, computer vision, natural language understanding, automated reasoning, and tools for design, manufacturing, and simulation of complex systems."[14]

Numerical and Scientific Simulation

The classic application for the iPSC/860 is the simulation of scientific experiments. Many problems in chemistry, physics, and biology are approached via simulation.

Most scientific simulation problems can be broken down into steps that involve local, independent computation followed by information exchange between processors.

For example, modeling an airflow over a wing can be done by placing a three-dimensional grid over the area to be simulated. For each block of the grid, airflow over the wing segment can be simulated almost independently of other blocks. Information needs to be exchanged between blocks only when a molecule of air moves from one block to another. The size of the blocks can be varied to accommodate the number of processors, the amount of memory, and the precision required. Each processor in the iPSC/860 could be given one (or several) blocks of the grid, and, for the most part, each would execute independently of the other. This would create a very efficient program.

Note that this is very close to the same programming model used for this problem on the MP-1 (even though the MP-1 is a SIMD machine). This shows the fundamental similarities that can exist between what appear on the surface to be radically different computers.

Financial Modeling

An interesting application area that fits the iPSC/860 is financial modeling. Many of the problems in this area require the solution of large systems of linear equations. This becomes a matrix manipulation problem. As with the simulation problem just described, matrix solvers can be programmed by breaking the matrices into blocks. Each block can be partially solved independently of the others. The ratio of information exchange with other nodes to computation time on each node is small, which means that such a problem is a good fit for a machine like the iPSC/860.

Other applications in the financial area involve performing the same calculation on thousands of different data sets. For example, analyzing a stock portfolio might require the same risk calculation on each stock in the portfolio. This is inherently parallel and is extremely well suited to the iPSC/860. Note that this works equally as well on a SIMD computer, since all the processors would be executing the same calculations. However, if the portfolio is more complex (such as having stocks, bonds, and options), then each processor would be executing a different type of calculation, depending on whether its data was a stock, bond, or option. This more complex application would not be as good a fit for a SIMD machine.

Teradata DBC/1012 Model 4

Teradata is a low-profile computer company that has been able to become one of the leading parallel processing companies. By sales, it is the largest parallel processing company; it was also the first. The company focuses on the design and manufacture of high-performance database machines. Most of their clients are Fortune 200 companies.

Product Line Description

The DBC/1012 Model 4 is the latest of the computer systems from Teradata. It is a distributed-memory MIMD computer with an interconnect different from any mentioned before, called *Ynet*, which will be described subsequently. The machine is designed to be a server on a network or a back-end database machine to a traditional mainframe. It is not used as a general-purpose computer.

History

Teradata Corporation was founded in 1979 to design and build high-performance relational database computers. This was five years before any other parallel processing company. It has grown at an incredible rate since shipping its first computer, in 1984. Teradata's first-generation machines were built around the Intel 8086, which made the machine highly underpowered. It was with the second generation, built using the Intel 80286, that the machines started making inroads into the commercial database market. Their latest machine uses the Intel 486 and is certainly the most powerful in the market. One of the machine's strengths is its ability to manage very large databases; while most traditional machines can only handle up to tens of gigabytes of data, the Teradata computers can handle up to hundreds of gigabytes. The largest installations have over 500 gigabytes of data online.

Company

The company (see Figure 4-12) is known for its low-profile approach in the parallel processing arena. It is not very visible in the parallel processing research community. It has focused on bringing parallel processing to a specific application area: relational database systems. Very few of the machines have been used for parallel processing research, unlike the computers mentioned previously. This may well have been an advantage, as the customer base of Teradata is composed of *Fortune* 200 companies, who generally take a low-risk, conservative approach to their information strategy. The other reason is that although the machine could be used as a general-purpose computer, it has found a niche as a special-purpose database server. This style of computing, called client/server computing, is just recently com-

Company	Teradata Corporation 101 North Sepulveda Boulevard El Segundo, CA 90245
Contact	Robin Tanchum Manager, Corporate Communications (213) 524-6162
Number of Employees	approx. 1500
Revenue (1991)	$258M
Product(s)	DBC/1012 Model 4, with 6 to over 1000 processors
Installed base (1991)	over 200 installations

Figure 4-12. *Teradata Corporation background*

ing into the mainstream, and this portends well for the company's future.

Classification and Block Diagram

The Teradata DBC/1012 Model 4 (Figure 4-13) is a classic MIMD distributed-memory computer. Because it is dedicated to one specific application—a database server—the components of the system are specialized. Three processor types exist: the communications processor (COP), the access module processor (AMP), and the interface processor (IFP). Each has special hardware and software to perform its function. The IFP provides an interface to a host computer. There can be more than one IFP, and they can be connected to the same or different hosts. The software on the computer keeps track of and manages database accesses from different hosts.

The COP is similar to the IFP, except that instead of being the interface to a host computer, the COP provides a network interface and remote system management. The COP is an Intel

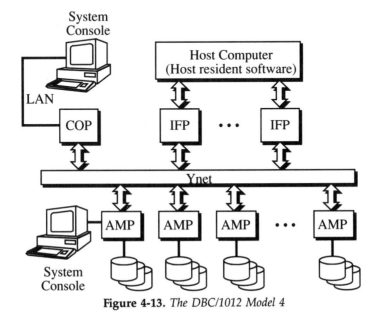

Figure 4-13. *The DBC/1012 Model 4*

486–based processing element with eight megabytes of RAM. Again, a DBC/1012 system can be configured with more than one COP to handle multiple networks.

The AMP is the primary workhorse of the DBC/1012, where the database query processing occurs. The AMP is an Intel 486 processor with eight megabytes of RAM. The AMP contains the disk controller, which interfaces to up to four disk drives. Each drive in the current model holds either 1.2 GB or 1.6 GB of data.

There can be up to 968 processors in a system. Normally, this is configured as a small number of COPs and IFPs and a larger number of AMPs.

The DBC/1012 functions by taking database requests, in DBC/SQL, from the host or workstations, processing them in the IFP or the COP, and then, through the Ynet, sending the specific relational operations that must be performed to the AMPs. The results are then accumulated by the IFP or the COP and sent back to the requesting computer.

The Ynet

The Ynet is slightly different from the interconnection networks described in Chapter 2. The networks described there had no logic of their own; any calculations or message routing was determined by the processors. The network was just the road on which the messages traveled. The Ynet actually has logic built into its switches, which is used to assist in routing messages to the correct AMP.

The Ynet is also used to perform sort/merge operations. When an ordered result is requested in the originating SQL statement, the individual AMPs will perform sorts on their portion of the results, and then the Ynet will perform the final merge operation as the messages are being sent back to the COP or the IFP. Benchmarks have shown that the Ynet is responsible for doubling the performance of the DBC/1012 on sort/merge operations.[15]

Software

The DBC/1012 has a complete suite of software tools for managing the database and the computer. These tools run variously on the system console, on a workstation, or on a host computer.

How Amdahl's Laws Are Addressed

As would be expected of a computer that is able to special-ize and is a commercial success, the DBC/1012 is well-balanced according to Amdahl's Laws (Figure 4-14). Peak processor per-formance is well matched to the memory size. It turns out that each AMP processor (the dominant processor type in the sys-tem) has a performance of nine MIPS and has eight megabytes of memory. This is almost perfect balance. Each processor also has a cache memory, which allows the processor to achieve its full potential. The I/O bandwidth is also well-tuned. Since each AMP is directly connected to the disks it manages, the Ynet is not involved in I/O and so is not a limiter. Here again, the I/O is well matched to the memory size and processor perfor-mance. If anything, the I/O is more robust than is needed for a

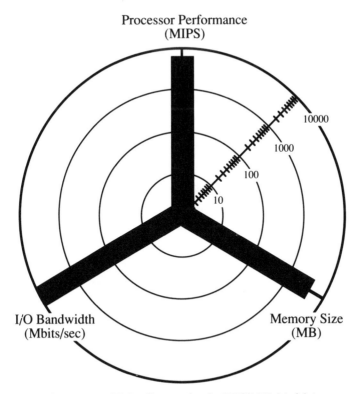

Figure 4-14. *Kiviat diagram for the DBC/1012 Model 4*

general-purpose computer, but for database processing this extra bandwidth is helpful.

Programming Model

As mentioned before, this machine is not used as a general-purpose computer, so the machine is not directly programmable. It is a relational database server designed to respond to fourth-generation languages such as SQL. Applications reside on host computers (either mainframes, directly connected via communication channels, or minicomputers, workstations, and PCs connected via local area networks). The applications, using a fourth-generation data access language, access information stored on the DBC/1012.

The parallelism is hidden from the programmers and user. The parallelism is extensively utilized by the database and communications software provided by Teradata.

What Changed to Make It Successful

Two changes helped propel this company forward. First, the computer changed the microprocessor from an Intel 8086 to an Intel 286. This cured a performance problem that the machine exhibited. The second change was environmental: The company was based on providing relational database systems, and it wasn't until the mid-to-late 1980s that relational databases came into major use.

Relational Database Systems

Relational database systems have a significant strength in their ability to be flexible. Older database systems (such as the hierarchical and network databases) delivered high performance for applications they were designed for, but for unexpected queries the older databases performed poorly. Relational databases, on the other hand, performed equally well on all queries. As companies moved into the information age, and executives started requesting and using decision support systems, RDBMS's were the systems of choice.

▼

MANAGING BY FACT—THE CITICORP WAY

All businesses can gain from managing by fact, and banks are no exception. To manage by fact, a company must have the appropriate information, and technology is the key to making it available. To accomplish this, Citicorp, one of the world's largest banks, is betting on parallel processing from Teradata.

Citicorp is a global banking corporation with more than 11 distinct banks and savings and loans as well as many overseas offices, with a long-term information strategy for integrating those businesses into a single information base. This would, for example, allow customers to bank at any of the diverse branches nationwide.

It would also give the bank the facts to better serve their customers. By merging all of the information about customer bank accounts, savings accounts, mortgages, credit cards, and so on, branch officers and market researchers can obtain a total picture of the financial position of the customer and be able to target specific bank products. For instance, a bank officer can select households, with children about to begin college, living in a 10-mile radius of the branch, who have taken out mortgages recently but don't have a home equity loan, and send specific mailings to them about home equity loans. Then, by tracking the responses to the mailings (since the customers targeted are known), the bank can determine the effectiveness of particular marketing campaigns, helping them to achieve continuous improvement.

One of the key advantages to Citicorp of going with a parallel processor is its ability to expand as the application demand grows. Adding more processors to the Teradata computer is almost as simple as bolting another cabinet in place. Benchmark results on Citibank's computers show that database performance effectively doubles as the number of processors and storage is doubled.

The primary computer complex for Citibank's consumer banking unit is composed of a large 168-processor DBC/1012, fed by two mainframes with banking transactions and other data. Currently, the Teradata machine keeps track of ATM transactions for six days and is updated by over 100 transactions per second. Altogether, Citicorp owns more than nine Teradata computers.

Source: Michelle Bekey, "Collecting Dividends on Data," Teradata Corporation, April 1990.

Teradata had recognized this shift early in the 1980s and designed the DBC/1012 to run an RDBMS very efficiently. They figured out how to execute the RDBMS in parallel, allowing a single query to be decomposed into requests to hundreds of processors and disks, and then to collect and consolidate the answers and present them back to the user. The efficiency of their RDBMS, together with its ability to store hundreds of gigabytes of information online, made the DBC/1012 an ideal machine for the information age.

Applications Well-Suited to This Machine

As the world moves from mainframe to desktop computing, the need for a central repository of the corporate information assets has not gone away; if anything, it has gotten stronger. But the central repository no longer needs to be a mainframe. The sole use of the repository (which might more appropriately be called an *information server* instead of a database server) would be to collect, distribute, and manage the terabytes that comprise the information assets of the company. In such an environment, the applications would reside on the desktop and would send requests to the information server. The requests would feed the results of the requests back into the desktop application for manipulation by the user.

For example, a spreadsheet application might be constructed by a bank manager interested in finding out how many households within a five-mile radius of her branch have incomes of $50,000 and average balances greater than $5000. With software available today, the spreadsheet can access a centralized information server through SQL and insert the data automatically into its calculations.

The Teradata DBC/1012, through the use of parallel processing, is well suited to this environment. Not only can individual queries be parallelized, but multiple requests from different clients can be handled simultaneously. This makes it ideal for client/server applications, where throughput and response time are both critical.

Summary

The third generation of parallel processors definitely learned from their predecessors. Many of the problems that had limited the applicability of parallel processors to the commercial world have been solved. Improvements in I/O capability and substantial performance achievements have made these machines attractive to the commercial marketplace. Companies are finding that they can improve their edge over the competition by taking advantage of applications in which these machines excel.

Key Points

1. Many of the deficiencies of the early generations of parallel processors have been corrected in the current commercially available machines.

2. Improvements have been made in programming environments and in I/O capability, which in third-generation systems is a better match to their processing performance.

3. The most significant achievement of the supercomputer-class parallel processors (like the iPSC/860 and the MP-1) has been to outperform traditional supercomputers, such as the Cray-2, on production applications.

4. Mid-range parallel processors such as the Sequent Symmetry can interconnect with existing machines to provide the scalability and performance necessary for demanding, information-intensive business applications.

5. At least one company has found a niche for a special-purpose parallel processor. Teradata's DBC/1012 is dedicated to being a relational database server, either as a back-end to a mainframe or as a server on a network.

References

1. *Symmetry Technical Reference Manual*, Sequent Computer Systems, 1991.

2. A. Garg, "Parallel STREAMS—A Multi-Processor Implementation," *Usenix Winter '90*, January 1990.

3. S. DeFazio, and J. Hull, "Toward Servicing Textual Database Transactions on Symmetric Shared-Memory Multiprocessors," *Proceedings, Fourth Interna-*

tional Workshop on High Performance Transaction Systems, Asilomar Conference Center, September 22–25, 1991.

4. T. Blank, "The MasPar MP-1 Architecture," *Proceedings of IEEE Compcon Spring 1990,* IEEE, February, 1990.

5. J. R. Nickolls, "The Design of the MasPar MP-1: A Cost Effective Massively Parallel Computer," *Proceedings of IEEE Compcon Spring 1990,* IEEE, February 1990.

6. P. Christy, "Software to Support Massively Parallel Computing on the MasPar MP-1," *Proceedings of IEEE Compcon Spring 1990,* IEEE, February 1990.

7. K. E. Batcher, "Design of a Massively Parallel Processor," *IEEE Transactions on Computers,* September 1980, pp. 836–840.

8. R. Grondalski, "A VLSI Chip Set for a Massively Parallel Architecture," *International Solid State Circuits Conference,* February 1987.

9. Kenneth P. Jacobsen, "Computational Fluid Dynamics: Application Note," MasPar Computer Corporation, 1990.

10. Kenneth P. Jacobsen, "Image Convolutions: Application Note," MasPar Computer Corporation, 1990.

11. Approval to reprint MasPar technical information has been granted by MasPar at our request for illustrative purposes only. MasPar assumes no responsibility for the context in which the information is being used, nor the currency of the data.

12. Intel Corporation.

13. Cray Research, Inc, *Cray Research Fact Sheet,* 1991.

14. Executive Office of the President, Office of Science and Technology Policy, *A Research and Development Strategy for High Performance Computing,* November 20, 1987.

15. Graham, Dan, "Linear Performance: Comparing the Architectures," *UNISPHERE,* November 1990.

5

Parallel Processors— New Releases

This generation of computers has a rendezvous with destiny.
adapted from Franklin D. Roosevelt, Address, 1936

The world does not stand still. Computer technology is moving at an extremely fast pace. This chapter looks at two of the latest parallel processors, from two of the leaders in parallel processing, Thinking Machines Corporation and Intel. Their new machines, the CM-5 and the Paragon, represent the current state-of-the-art in extremely high-performance computing.

At an industry conference in November 1991, Thinking Machines Corporation announced its next generation, the CM-5, to be available in early 1992. The machine can be configured with over 16,000 processors, with a combined performance of 352,000 MIPS and 2048 GFLOPS (2 teraflops).

At that same conference, Intel announced its Paragon computer, to be available by the middle of 1992. The machine is capable of delivering up to 300 GFLOPS and 160,000 MIPS with a full complement of 4000 processor nodes.

The race continues.

Changes in the Industry

The computer industry has been changing over the past three years. More and more companies are defining their next-generation systems in terms of parallel processing. The leaders in the performance race are Thinking Machines and Intel, but IBM and Cray Research have both announced that parallel processing will be part of a future product. Cray Research has an ongoing project to deliver a massively parallel processor during 1993.

AND WHAT ABOUT CRAY?

Not to give up the mantle of the world's supercomputing champion, Cray Research announced a 16-processor Cray Y-MP C90 in late November, 1991. By using multiple processing units, this machine is capable of 16 GFLOPS of performance.

Continuing the parallel processing revolution, Cray Research has started development of a microprocessor-based parallel processor, with the first product expected in 1993.[1] They will be using a new microprocessor, by DEC, which attains the world-shattering speed of 200 MFLOPS. This chip, designed by Dick Sites, is proof that microprocessors will be the main processing units of everything from desktops to supercomputers. Even Cray Research acknowledges that each of the new chips has the power of a Cray-1.

Source: Cray Research Corporation.

Thinking Machines Corporation CM-5

The CM-5[2] is the latest entry into the parallel processing arena by Thinking Machines Corporation. This new design is meant to survive for most of the 1990s and to deliver one of the major milestones of computing—reaching a teraflop of sustained performance.

WHAT IS A TERAFLOP?

A teraflop is simply one measure of performance of a computer. It means that a computer can perform one trillion (1,000,000,000,000) floating-point operations per second (FLOPS). It is equal to 1000 gigaFLOPS or one million megaFLOPS. Looking at it slightly differently, the first Cray-1 had a peak speed of 160 MFLOPS, so a teraflop computer is 6250 times as fast. The first IBM PCs had a performance of one-tenth of a megaflop, so a teraflop computer is 10 million times as fast (equal to the combined performance of 10 million IBM PCs working together on a single problem).

What is amazing about a computer reaching this performance level by the mid-1990s is that in only twenty years, the performance of the best computers will have increased by a factor approaching ten thousand, and the cost of one of the best computers will be no more than what it was in 1975! It is hard to find anything else in this world that has been able to achieve that price/performance decrease in that small of a time period.

The Company

Thinking Machines Corporation (see Figure 5-1) was started in 1983 to develop and market high-performance computers based on parallel processing. The original concept for its machines came from the MIT dissertation of Thinking Machines' founding scientist, Daniel Hillis.

Product Description

Thinking Machines has been known for its SIMD approach to parallelism. Both the CM-1 and the CM-2 were SIMD machines, and they espoused the data parallelism philosophy (Chapter 7) in both hardware and software. The new CM-5, however, is a MIMD machine, and it is based on conventional microprocessors,

Company	Thinking Machines Corporation 245 First Street Cambridge, MA 02142
Contact	Tim Browne (617) 234-5525
Number of Employees (1991)	approx. 450
Revenue (1991)	not publicly disclosed
Product(s)	CM-2, CM-5, DataVault
Installed base (1991)	more than 60

Figure 5-1. *Thinking Machines Corporation background*

as opposed to Thinking Machines' early proprietary designs. This means that this architecture will be able to take advantage of the same technology that is used by most of the other parallel processor vendors. As was pointed out in Chapter 3, the fact that SIMD machines had to rely on proprietary microprocessor designs was a serious detriment to their existence. Thinking Machines' CM-5 seems to prove the point.

Figure 5-2 shows the basic structure of the CM-5. There are three types of processing nodes in the design. The P nodes are for application processing; the CP nodes are for system administration, program development, and I/O administration; and the I/O nodes are interfaces to specific I/O devices (such as disks, tapes, and graphics).

Each of the P processing nodes is based around a SPARC microprocessor. With current technology, this gives each processor 22 MIPS of performance. The organization of the processors is important. The P nodes are designed to execute the application. They each contain up to 32 MB of local memory, and a floating-point accelerator can be added to boost the floating-point performance of a P node to 128 MFLOPS.

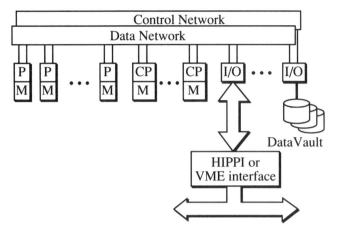

Figure 5-2. *The CM-5*

The CP nodes are architecturally similar to the P nodes, but they run system software, including a complete operating system (a version of UNIX). They are designed to provide the user interface and the resource management of the parallel processor. All I/O resource allocation goes through these processors. User control of an application must also pass through the CP nodes.

The I/O nodes are unique in that they can connect to multiple network links. This enables the effective bandwidth of communication from the parallel processors to the I/O interface to be faster than the bandwidth of a single link in the network. For example, each link in the network can sustain from 5 to 20 megabytes per second of communication. A HIPPI (high-performance peripheral interface) can handle 100 megabytes of data per second, so the HIPPI I/O node uses six network links to connect to the parallel processors. This is a different approach from that used by the MasPar MP-1, where the I/O RAM achieved the same result by providing a randomly addressed buffer between the I/O devices and the parallel processors. It remains to be seen which works better.

The CM-5 has two communication networks, the Data Network and the Control Network. The Data Network is passive and has the same function as the network in the iPSC/860 and in the Paragon (discussed later in this chapter). Messages between processing nodes (P, CP, or I/O) pass through the Data Network.

The Control Network is not a passive network; it is more like the Ynet of the Teradata DBC/1012. That is, the Control Network has computational logic built into it to perform special functions on messages as they travel. It is optimized for certain types of common data-parallel operations (such as synchronizing processing nodes, broadcasting, and combining values from different nodes to produce a single result). This will give the machine a slight edge in performance for a small number of applications over parallel processors without this capability, but the additional cost involved in designing and manufacturing this additional network may not be justified over time.

How Amdahl's Laws Are Addressed

Figure 5-3 shows the balance of the system. It is actually difficult to determine the balance because of the flexibility of the I/O subsystem. The scalability of the I/O, as well as the ability to vary the number of P nodes and I/O nodes, makes determining a maximum I/O bandwidth difficult. But the system is designed to support enough I/O to provide a balanced system as shown. Take, for instance, a 16,000-processor CM-5. The peak performance is 352,000 MIPS. The I/O bandwidth necessary to provide a balanced system would be 44,000 megabytes per second, 1760 DataVault units, or 440 HIPPI interfaces. The architecture supports such a system; building and housing such a system would be a challenge.

The memory is well matched with the integer performance of the P node. The floating-point performance (not shown), on the other hand, is somewhat out of balance. When the floating-point accelerator is added to the system, the peak floating-point performance is 2048 gigaFLOPS, while the memory does not grow beyond 384 billion bytes. So, according to Amdahl's Laws, the floating-point performance will be memory-starved, limiting the peak performance on many applications.

Programming Model

The programming model developed by Thinking Machines for the CM-5 is for the machine to be configured into partitions,

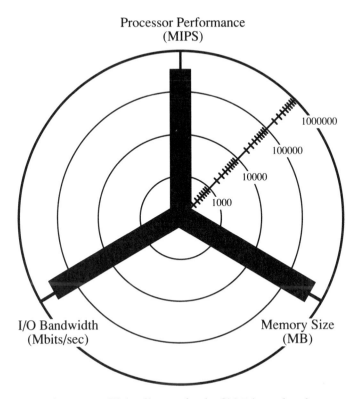

Figure 5-3. *Kiviat diagram for the CM-5 (note that the scale is 1000 times that of previous Kiviat diagrams)*

with each partition being assigned a set of P nodes (minimum of 32) under the control of a CP node. At least with the current design, the partitions are relatively static, changing maybe only two or three times a day. This is reminiscent of the early multitasking operating systems from IBM, where fixed partitions of memory were created by the system administrator and programs had to fit in them. These memory partitions only changed a few times a day. The partitions of these old operating systems gave way to virtual memory. It is reasonable to assume that over time, the concept of virtual processors will allow more efficient management of the CM-5 parallel processor (or its successors).

Note that the CP node has the same function as the front-end processor in earlier parallel processors. This means that application development does not get the advantage of the parallel processor. A big improvement over earlier machines is the tight integration of the front end (in this case the CP) into the system. For example, all of the I/O for the machine uses the same, highly parallel, I/O subsystem (the I/O nodes). This alleviates one of the significant bottlenecks in the earlier machines.

Intel Paragon

In November of 1991, Intel announced the Paragon XP/S, a successor to the iPSC/860 (Chapter 4), which will begin shipments during 1992. The Paragon XP/S[3] computer system is a refinement of the distributed-memory MIMD architecture exhibited by the iPSC/860.

Between the iPSC/860 and the Paragon XP/S, fundamental improvements have been made in the interconnect and the operating system. The interconnect between the processors achieves a data transfer rate of 200 megabytes per second. This makes the Paragon a much more balanced system than the iPSC/860. Furthermore, the operating system now runs on the parallel processor, as in the highly successful Sequent Symmetry, thus obviating the need for a front-end computer.

The Paragon computer is going to be the major architecture for Intel for at least the next five years. One interesting thing to note is the similarities between the CM-5 and the Paragon. They are much more alike than they are different.

Product Description

The Paragon is still a MIMD machine, with an attempt to be as homogeneous as possible with respect to the nodes. Instead of having different functions for different processors (such as the P and the CP nodes of the CM-5), the Paragon has only one type of processing node. In Figure 5-4, the P and the S nodes are processing nodes, with the difference being how they are being used at any given moment. The S node is a service node, meaning that it is responsible for running user interfaces or controlling

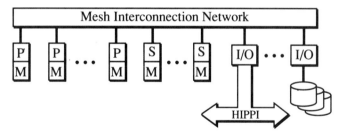

Figure 5-4. *The Paragon*

I/O devices. At any time, it can be reallocated to run parallel applications.

Since the processing nodes run a standard version of UNIX (OSF/1 with some parallel extensions), performance could be degraded for parallel applications. This is avoided by using a processing node design that was pioneered in the Loral Dataflo[4] computer in 1984. Each processing node has two microprocessors. One of the processors is dedicated to running the operating system and handling all the message passing. In this way the second processor can run the parallel application without interruption. Since the two processors share a common memory, adding the second processor is fairly inexpensive, and it performs special data-parallel operations instead of relying on special logic in the network as in the CM-5.

The I/O for the Paragon is handled through special I/O nodes. Different nodes provide SCSI, HIPPI, and VME interfaces. Each provides up to a 200-megabyte-per-second interface into the interconnection network (bidirectional; it carries 100 megabytes per second each way). Operating system software provides a file interface to the I/O nodes to allow multiple nodes to participate as a single I/O device.

How Amdahl's Laws Are Addressed

Figure 5-5 shows the Kiviat diagram for the Paragon computer. The most notable area is the I/O performance, which is much less (by a factor of five) than is necessary to support the full performance over a wide range of applications. For example, the

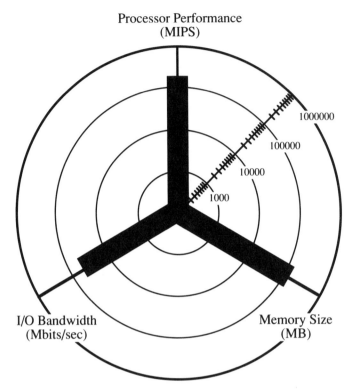

Figure 5-5. *Kiviat diagram for the Paragon (note that the scale is 1000 times that of the Kiviat diagrams in previous chapters)*

I/O bandwidth of the Teradata DBC/1012 (Chapter 4) is actually greater than required by Amdahl's Laws (it is tuned for high-performance database applications, which are I/O-intensive).

Programming Model

The Paragon has a compatibility mode, which allows applications developed on the iPSC/860 to run. This is accomplished by the Paragon using the same message-passing library as the iPSC/860. There is also a new set of parallel processing subroutines, which are part of the OSF/1 parallel processing release. Figure 5-6 shows the programming model of the system.

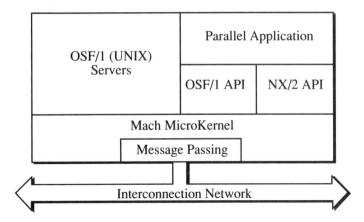

Figure 5-6. *The Paragon programming model*

One of the significant advantages of the Paragon over other parallel processors is that the parallel applications run in virtual memory. This means that applications can use more memory than exists on a node. This helps substantially with scalability.

Another feature is the use of *Shared Virtual Memory*, which is a software-only implementation of a virtual memory system, which allows a program to use a shared-memory model for programming. As was have seen in the success of the Sequent Symmetry, this programming model makes parallel programming very simple. The Paragon software ensures data consistency, which is similar to cache coherency (Chapter 3). On the Paragon, though, because it is a software-only implementation, the performance of the shared-memory programming model is substantially worse than message-passing. Note that this is not the case for real shared-memory systems, such as the Sequent Symmetry, where the hardware-assisted shared memory allows communication and synchronization at memory access speeds with essentially no latency. On the Paragon, the communication and synchronization required by the shared-virtual-memory programming model is actually layered software on top of software-based message-passing mechanisms. This leads to significant inefficiencies and will probably not be used except in rare instances.

Summary

The Thinking Machines Corporation CM-5 and the Intel Paragon definitely foreshadow the future. Both machines are becoming more general-purpose, getting rid of the front-end computers and using standard operating systems that run on the parallel processors. Both offer peak performance an order of magnitude greater than what is achievable with conventional sequential computers.

Interestingly, the two computers described here seem to be converging in general architecture. The programming models offered by the two machines are not that different, and, as was foretold in Chapter 1, the performance of the machines, even though built with different processors and with different interconnect technology, is roughly the same. The hypothesis of an underlying physics of computation is still viable.

Businesses are already lining up to put this new competitive tool to good use. American Express has stated its intention to purchase two CM-5s as a key element of its information-processing strategy. Prudential Securities (Chapter 6) is one of the first companies to announce its intent to upgrade their iPSC/860 to a Paragon machine during 1992.

The competition in the race to use these new machines for a business advantage is getting as fierce as that in the computer industry itself.

Key Points

1. Most major computer companies have announced projects to bring parallel processors to market.

2. The two latest machines from Thinking Machines Corporation and Intel reach performances approaching one teraflop, which represents a thousandfold increase in performance over what was available in 1990.

3. Both architectures are developing a more general-purpose capability, which makes them even more applicable to the commercial information systems organizations.

4. Companies are no longer waiting to run experiments on the new computers. Major companies like American Express and Prudential Securities are standing in line to buy large configurations of the machines, even before they are ready to ship.

References

1. Russell Mitchell, "What? Cray Computers Eating Dust?" *Business Week,* November 25, 1991, p. 88.

2. Thinking Machines Corporation, "The Connection Machine CM-5 Technical Summary," October 1991.

3. Intel Corporation, "Paragon XP/S Product Overview," 1991.

4. J. Van Zandt, I. Kaplan, and G. Williamson, "The LORAL DATAFLO System," presented at the Second SIAM Conference on Parallel Processing for Scientific Computing, November 18, 1985.

6

Application Domains

Each morning sees some task begun,
Each evening sees it close;
Something attempted, something done,
Has earned a night's repose.
Longfellow, *The Village Blacksmith*

The most recent generation of parallel processors is making inroads into the production environments of major corporations. The reason is simple: Parallel processing gives companies a competitive edge in business.

This chapter will present two case studies in which parallel processors are making a significant difference. The first is about US West NewVector Group, Incorporated (USWNVG), a large subsidiary of US West. USWNVG is building its information management system around both an MVS mainframe environment and a shared-memory MIMD parallel processor.

Then we'll look at Prudential Securities, Incorporated, which is using a distributed-memory MIMD parallel processor to decrease response time dramatically on securities trade analyses, decreasing its risks and increasing its profits.

US West NewVector Group, Incorporated

USWNVG was formed in 1984 to provide paging and cellular phone service to 14 Western states and several foreign countries, including St. Petersburg, Russia.

The Business Environment

USWNVG started its information system in 1983 with a set of PCs for desktop use and a service bureau to provide an order-and-billing system and a financials package. The original applications were based on a hierarchial database and an IBM mainframe. As the company was growing at the phenomenal rate of 70 percent per year, it quickly outgrew the canned applications and needed to do more customization of the applications and provide better control of production quality. To accommodate this growth, USWNVG purchased an IBM 4381 and moved the service bureau applications inhouse, where customization and production operations could be done more easily (Figure 6-1). This was in 1985.

The number of applications that were necessary to support the rapidly growing business also grew at an exponential rate. Systems were needed to support market analysis, financial reporting, payroll, inventory tracking, budgeting and financial modeling, collections, and credit card validation. One of the main problems with a hierarchical database is its inflexibility in accommodating significant changes to the database structure. This inflexibility was the exact opposite of what USWNVG needed. The demands of the new applications required major database changes. The programming staff at USWNVG was not able to

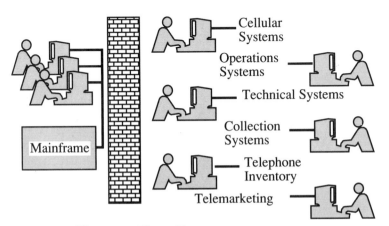

Figure 6-1. *The problem: no system integration*

respond quickly enough to the demand for new and modified applications. And with a company growing at 70 percent per year, you don't stop the growth—you improvise. As always happens in this situation, individual departments started purchasing standalone systems to solve their immediate problems. And since these systems were not integrated into the main computing environment, requested changes to the total system took even longer to implement. The standalone systems solved localized problems, but did not work in harmony to create an optimized global solution for the company.

A small company can get by with fewer processes than a large company; ad hoc solutions work because there are a limited number of communication channels. As a company grows, communication channels grow exponentially. Institutionalizing business processes that have been in people's heads becomes critical for the company's survival. The information systems that served the company well in the early days no longer work for the expanded company.

Factors Influencing the Decision to Go Parallel

By late 1988, according to John Black, Systems Architect at USWNVG, the information systems development projects at USWNVG were backlogged by six to nine months. The company was still growing at a rate of over 70 percent a year and facing an information vacuum. USWNVG information system professionals recognized this and started to change. They decided to redesign their information systems so they could catch up with the company and be ready for continued growth. The goal was an information infrastructure that would allow ultimate flexibility while delivering information services in a timely, cost-effective manner. The new system had to be all of the following:

- Based on open systems and a client-server model
- Flexible in information system structure
- Scalable to accommodate international business
- Integrable with MVS systems

Based on Open Systems

The *open systems* approach was selected by USWNVG to give the company the greatest capability to ride the wave of technology as the company grew. Open systems allow the greatest flexibility in terms of system platforms. They also provide application interfaces that enable the use of a wide range of off-the-shelf applications.

Flexible

A company growing at the rate of 70 percent a year is going through rapid changes, which require an information system that can accommodate change in a timely fashion. This translates to flexibility in the structure of the software and hardware.

Scalable

One of the unique aspects of the USWNVG business is its focus on national and international markets. National and international regulations require separate systems in each country. Export restrictions limit system size in some countries. Scalability is imperative for decentralized systems of different sizes. The same applications should run unchanged on small systems that handle the USWNVG service area for St. Petersberg, Russia, or on large systems that manage the entire US service area. Each system should be able to grow over time with minimal upgrade cost.

Integrable

In order not to disrupt the ongoing business, and to allow the best of both worlds, the new system had to integrate with the existing MVS environment, as well as provide a platform for running and integrating the standalone systems. This would allow the easy migration to the new environment, without the "all or nothing" risks that would attend a complete replacement of the MVS systems.

The Solution System

The key components of the system USWNVG chose to complement its MVS environment were a relational database management system (RDBMS), a UNIX operating system, and a shared-memory MIMD parallel processor. Relational databases currently provide the most flexibility in developing information system applications. By going to a relational database, USWNVG expected to understand its data better, to be more prepared for change, and to reduce the application development backlog. In short, it expected to be more flexible, which is of great strategic importance.

Oracle was chosen as the RDBMS provider on Unix, DB2 on MVS. A Sequent Symmetry 2000 was chosen to host the RDBMS, because it is open, is scalable from single-processor to mainframe performance, and offers the highest RDBMS performance of any open system.

USWNVG requirements were a perfect match for the capabilities of a parallel processor. As discussed in Chapter 4, the system demands of relational databases and the client-server application model are easily handled by shared-memory MIMD parallel machines such as the Sequent Symmetry 2000. In fact, parallel processors were the key to drastically reducing the price/performance of RDBMS's in the mid-1980s, bringing relational databases to the forefront of the industry.

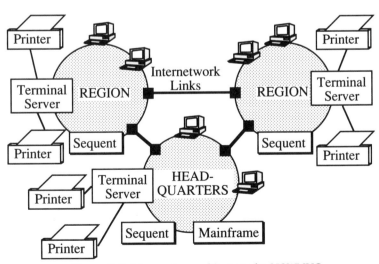

Figure 6-2. *New system architecture for USWNVG*

Scalability, and especially incremental upgrading, is a unique feature of all parallel processors. It allows a company's computing demand to grow without huge initial investments and without the loss of entry-level systems.

The complete USWNVG information system (Figure 6-2) is composed of many Sequent Symmetry parallel processors. Just as important in the picture are the legacy IBM-compatible mainframe, which still holds important data, and the desktop PC systems. Open systems provide the capability to integrate dissimilar systems with ease. Although not fault-tolerant, the Sequent parallel processors provide enough reliability and availability to accommodate a 7-day-a-week, 24-hour-a-day system requirement. This same system, on varying scales, is replicated by USWNVG throughout the world in its installations.

Integrating into the Environment

To fit into the USWNVG information system, the parallel processor computer had to have an architecture based on standards such as an SQL-oriented database, a TCP/IP Ethernet, the UNIX operating system, ANSI C, POSIX IEEE 1003.1, and X-Windows. The system had to connect to the IBM-compatible mainframe and to PCs. Even though there are many UNIX suppliers, the interoperability between different versions is not perfect. For this reason, USWNVG decided to standardize on a single UNIX platform—the Sequent Symmetry.

Also, parallel processor software is not as mature as software for the traditional mainframes. This is especially true for large system management functions like backup and restore, network management, and system configuration monitoring and management. In these areas USWNVG either went without many of the standard mainframe features, left the applications on the mainframe, or wrote its own. For instance, USWNVG has written its own tape management application.

Application Development

Developing applications for the Sequent parallel processor was not any more difficult than development for a conventional com-

A CASE IN POINT

US West NewVector Group has been growing at a phenomenal rate since 1984. As is customary in the cellular phone business, customers are provided access to phone services and billed at the end of each month. A normal part of doing business this way is the continual accumulation of bad debt. USWNVG's bad debt had been holding steady at a rate of $20,000 per month. This was low enough to appear completely under control.

Then it hit $500,000 in one month.

Management attention was immediately directed to the problem. The entire information system supporting new accounts had be to changed. New account activation would have to provide instantaneous credit approval at the same time that new service was being processed by sales people. The challenge was to put together a system to manage new account information in a way that would process thousands (and later tens of thousands) of new accounts every day. And because bad debt was growing, the system had to be changed right away.

The scenario was a chief information officer's worst nightmare: changing a complex information system overnight.

However, USWNVG found a quick solution. They modified the new account system, established a computer-to-computer connection to a credit bureau, and began to collect and process credit information as part of establishing each new account. All of these changes took place within 60 days after the first sign of a problem and only 45 days after the identification of a solution. The rapid solution would have been impossible under their previous nonopen, nonflexible, nonparallel system.

Not only was the bad debt problem brought under control, but the new system was able to target the customers that the company wanted, thus generating sales leads. So the system not only saved money, but made money—the best of all solutions.

This solution was possible only because of talented people, the strategic vision of the information specialists to use flexible information systems, and the power of parallel processors.

puter. Most application development was in C and SQL. Since most of the parallelism was at the multiprocessing level and the database level, programmers did not have to specify parallelism directly to take advantage of it.

The biggest challenge was not in dealing with parallel processing but in converting from MVS/COBOL to Oracle/C/UNIX programming. Although some experienced UNIX programmers were hired, the vast majority of USWNVG programmers were retrained. This turned out to take longer than the two weeks anticipated. The USWNVG believes that three months is probably a more reasonable amount of time for the retraining effort, which should include the development of at least one system under the tutelage of an experienced UNIX programmer.

Lessons Learned

USWNVG took a calculated risk when they decided to go with parallel processing. John Black calls the years 1988 to 1991 "the ride down the razor blade," referring to the sharp learning curve the company endured. Experience has shown that it was the right decision at the right time. The company has continued to grow at 40 percent to 70 percent a year, and the information systems have grown along with the company.

A relational database approach was also a good choice. The data-modeling discipline imposed by relational systems improved USWNVG's ability to extract information from its systems and to make better decisions about the business. The parallel processor that made the choice feasible has allowed the company to grow its database to match its business needs.

As with almost any computer system, hardware was not the dominant headache. Converting from a proprietary shop to an open-systems shop (MVS and UNIX) was mainly a software and people challenge. Retraining programmers from MVS/COBOL to UNIX/C/SQL was a major undertaking, and keeping a heterogeneous operating environment, containing both the legacy and the UNIX systems, did not merely double the complexity; it exponentially increased it.

The major unexpected challenge was scaling the software. The hardware scaled well from small to large systems; some software applications did not. This was most true in the system management arena, where tools that work well for 5 to 10 gigabytes of data are useless for hundreds of gigabytes. While a network of 50 to 100 users can be managed effectively, managing a network of thousands of users requires a different type of software (which is not yet available off-the-shelf).

Prudential Securities, Inc.

Prudential Securities, Incorporated is one of the major securities firms on Wall Street. It was the first firm on Wall Street to purchase a parallel supercomputer and put it into production use.

The Business Environment

The business of securities trading is highly competitive[1] and full of risks. At any moment, a securities firm may hold hundreds of millions of dollars worth of securities, bought with the firm's money, with no identified buyer. Because of timing, the firm may have bought tens of millions of dollars worth of bonds only to see the market for them start to drop. But where there are risks there are rewards, and the bigger the risks, the bigger the rewards.

The Financial Strategies Group at Prudential was formed in the mid-1980s as part of Prudential's push into the fixed-income securities market. The firm believed that by having a state-of-the-art information system, it could reduce its risks and increase its profits.

Prudential started with a Digital Equipment Corporation VAX— which grew to two, then three, then became a VAX-Cluster. The firm used relational databases to manage the information and programmed in C. When those systems became too crowded or slow, the firm put Sun workstations on traders' and analysts' desks.

A major goal of computer systems in this environment is to reduce the risks, usually by modeling and intricate calculations. The compute power needed to analyze a transaction fully is truly awesome. For example, a complete calculation on a collateral transaction takes 16,000 minutes on a VAX 8800; on a three-processor Cray X-MP it runs in 100 minutes.[2]

Along with risk reduction, timing is critical. In some cases, the complex mathematics take too long to be useful. When a collateralized mortgage-backed obligation (CMO) is offered, the profitability analysis must be completed in time for a bid to be made; otherwise, the trader must go on intuition or not bid at all. On Wall Street, since all of the action occurs on computer screens, this trading has been called *screen warfare*. Without adequate high-performance computer support, the risks may outweigh the reward. In 1988, Prudential's VAX 6440 took several minutes to analyze a CMO offering, which meant that the trader had to hang up the phone, wait for the computer to produce the results, and then call back with a bid (if it was determined profitable). The delay between offer and bid could mean losing the deal to a competitor or losing contact with the offeror. Either way, time and money were being lost.

Factors Influencing the Decision

According to Dr. David Audley, a Director in the Financial Strategies Group, Prudential started looking in mid-1988 for additional ways to increase its compute power—to provide it with a competitive edge. The firm evaluated processors that would attach to its existing computers; evaluated application accelerators; and even ran benchmarks on a Cray. None of these seemed to provide the capabilities at the price Prudential was willing to pay.

The information system had already been designed as a client/server architecture, with the clients being workstations and PCs on a desktop, and the VAX's being used as computation servers. Prudential had even programmed its own "compute manager" to manage the distribution of the computation work load invisibly. This meant that whatever computer was selected, it should integrate smoothly into the overall information system as a compute server.

Audley had the primary financial applications analyzed, and discovered that the applications were highly parallel. This led Prudential to look for parallel-processor solutions. According to Audley, there were four major criteria for the solution system: performance; integration with existing systems; ease of programming; and no technological risk.

Performance
The machine had to have the potential to be at least ten times more powerful than the VAX Prudential was using. This was to guarantee the long-term viability of the strategy to go with a parallel processor.

Ability to Integrate with Existing Systems
The parallel processor had to integrate with the existing MIS computing environment. For Prudential, this meant that the machine had to work with an IBM mainframe, several VAX computers, and a plethora of workstations and PCs. The parallel processor was going to be a compute server, taking requests from the other computers and returning results, with no direct user interaction. It also meant that the computer had to be multitasking and capable of handling more than one request at a time.

Ease of Programming
It was critical that Prudential's programmers be able to develop applications for the parallel processor without significant retraining. The firm did not want to make its existing programmers obsolete, as they understood the securities business.

No Technological Risks
Any investment of this magnitude had to be guaranteed to work. The major investment was not going to be in the computer itself but in training and development of applications for the machine. That investment had to be protected. Prudential wanted to do business with a company that was going to be around to provide service, and evolve the parallel processor to remain competitive.

The Solution

In late 1988, Prudential decided to take the parallel plunge. The solution system was a 32-node Intel iPSC/2 (since upgraded to an iPSC/860). With this system, the CMO analysis, which took minutes on the VAX, can be performed in about 30 seconds, quick enough for the trader to stay on the phone during an offer and bid.

The first real production system was an adjustable-rate mortgage analysis system, which was up and running in early 1989. Over the next two years, all of the mortgage analysis programs were ported to the Intel computer.

Did the parallel processor help? In the first year of operation, the dollar volume of their mortgage-backed securities business quadrupled.

Integrating into the System

The iPSC/860 is a back end to the other computers in the networked environment—the computational workhorse for the network. Brokers, connected to the system through either a workstation, a PC, or a dumb terminal, select program options and execute operations with no knowledge of the actual location of the computation. Certain computations migrate from the VAX and workstations to the Intel parallel processor, at which point the iPSC/860 may request additional data from the VAX-based databases. The computations proceed, and the results are sent back to the brokers.

According to Audley, the integration as a compute server went extremely easily, far easier than had been expected. The "compute manager" was ported within the first week the machine was installed. The integration is through an Ethernet connected to the System Resource Manager (SRM) of the iPSC/860 (see Figure 4-10). The compute manager runs on the SRM, does the allocation of processors to the various applications, and performs all of the communication with the other computers.

With this complex client/server architecture, Prudential is able to execute several applications in real time. In one application that computes an adjustable-rate mortgage pricing model, the program that previously ran on a VAX in 5 to 10 minutes now runs in 14 seconds on an 8-node subset of the iPSC/860. This means that four brokers can run this application simultaneously on the 32-node machine. The added performance directly converts to customer satisfaction—and higher profits.

RISK AND REWARD

One of the latest applications to be ported to the iPSC/860 parallel processor at Prudential is its risk management system. This system is used to monitor in real time the trading position of the company and its risk exposure. Previous to this the system was run on a VAX. Even though the VAX was receiving trading information in real time, it was not fast enough to keep track of the risk exposure in real time. As the day progressed, the VAX kept getting farther and farther behind. Usually it was not until late in the evening that Prudential could determine what its exposure was at the end of the trading day. Now, with the Intel parallel processor, the firm is never more than a few minutes behind, and so can monitor its risk exposure continually.

According to Dr. David Audley, this ability is unique on Wall Street, and the value of being able to know and manage Prudential's exposure in real time is worth far more than the money made by any other application on the iPSC/860.

Application Development

One of the biggest surprises was the ease with which programmers learned to write parallel programs. Within the first day of operation, one programmer had ported a financial analysis package to the iPSC/2. Within the week, the package had been parallelized.

All of the application development is done in C and Fortran, using the parallel libraries that Intel supplies with the machine.

The porting model that Prudential uses is straightforward. First, port the application to a single node of the computer. This works out the compiler incompatibilities. Then go parallel, usually to only a two-node parallel program. In parallel computers (unlike in inductive reasoning in mathematics), if it works for two, it works for all.

Prudential has found that parallel programming is easy.

Lessons Learned

Prudential originally thought the major risks with basing its information system on a parallel processor would be that: the technology was not mature enough for production use and that the integration of the computer into the networked environment would be difficult. Both perceived risks turned out to be untrue. The machine has easily stood the test of production use since 1989, and the integration into the network was easy.

In fact, the area in which Prudential least expected problems— the performance—turned out to be the most problematic. As with all computers, compilers have a dramatic impact on the performance of applications on a machine. The original compilers for the Intel parallel processors caused the performance of the iPSC/860 to be far below what the hardware was capable of. It took several generations of compilers for the performance of the computer to meet expectations. These problems have now all gone away.

One of the most exciting events occurred when the firm upgraded the iPSC/2 to an iPSC/860. The Intel field service engineer walked in with a box full of iPSC/860 node boards. He turned off the iPSC/2, pulled out the i386-based nodes, and replaced them with the i860-based boards. Then he turned the computer on, loaded new system software, and left. That afternoon, all the applications for the machine were recompiled and executed. The results, with no change in the applications, was a fourfold increase in performance! The scalability and upgradability of parallel processing had proven itself in probably the first production environment for parallel supercomputers.

Where does all this go? According to Dr. David Audley, "Parallel processors are now crucial to stay competitive in the securities markets." Prudential has already announced that it will be upgrading to the next generation of parallel supercomputers from Intel when they become available.

Acknowledgments

I especially want to thank US West NewVector Group and Prudential Securities for their assistance in the preparation of this chapter.

At USWNVG, John Black, Systems Architect, was extremely helpful in explaining its success in redesigning its information system around a parallel processor. Greg Kleven at Sequent Computer Systems provided information about the installation.

At Prudential Securities, Dr. David Audley provided invaluable assistance in describing Prudential's experiences in putting a parallel processor into a production environment. Wendy Vittori, Director of Marketing at Intel Supercomputer Systems Division, helped by providing background information on the Prudential system.

References

1. Michael Lewis, *Liar's Poker,* W. W. Norton & Company, New York, 1989.
2. Dwight B. Davis, "Intel Woos Business Users," *Datamation,* May 1, 1991, pp. 34–38.

7

Programming
Parallel Processors

They are waiting on the shingle—will you come and join the dance?
Will you, won't you, will you, won't you, will you join the dance?
Will you, won't you, will you, won't you, won't you join the dance?
Lewis Carroll, *Alice's Adventures in Wonderland*

Parallel programming has been going on for many years; in the earlier days, it was called multiprocessing or multitasking. Parallel programming is not as difficult as it used to be. Programmers are finding that many applications are naturally parallel, and there are simple methods for decomposing programs to run effectively on a parallel processor.

The basic concept behind all parallel programming is that an application is really composed of a number of parts. While some parts are dependent on others, they are also independent of still others. If two parts are independent, they can be executed in parallel.

Coarse-Grain and Fine-Grain Parallelism

One word used to describe the style of parallelism is *granularity*. This refers to the number of computer instructions that are executed sequentially between communication and synchronization points with other processors. The endpoints of the granularity continuum are called *coarse grain* and *fine grain* (Figure 7-1).

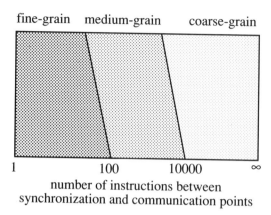

Figure 7-1. *Coarse- and fine-grain parallelism*

For coarse-grained programs, thousands (or millions) of lines of code are executed between communication and synchronization points. At the other end of the spectrum, fine-grained parallelism means that every instruction requires synchronization and communication with another processor. Coarse-grained parallelism is normally less complex, because for a program of a given number of lines of code there are fewer synchronization and communication points to be concerned with. Because of this, coarse-grained parallel programming is considered easier than fine-grained parallel programming.

Architectural Biases Toward Coarse or Fine Grain

Some architectures are more naturally programmed and offer more efficiency at a particular level of granularity (Figure 7-2). For example, the iPSC/860 is best programmed in a coarse-grained manner because of the performance cost of passing a message between two processors, which is due in part to the speed of the interconnection network and in part to the operating system overhead. If the iPSC/860 is programmed with only a few instructions between the sending and the receiving of a message, the performance of the machine will be only a small fraction of the potential performance. This is true of most distributed-memory MIMD machines.

Parallel Processor	Optimal Granularity
BBN Butterfly, TC2000	medium grain, coarse grain
Thinking Machines CM-1, CM-2	fine grain
Active Memory Technology DAP	fine grain
Intel iPSC/860	medium grain, coarse grain
Meiko Computing Surface	medium grain, coarse grain
MasPar MP-1	fine grain
nCUBE nCUBE/2	medium grain, coarse grain
Sequent Symmetry 2000	fine grain, coarse grain

Figure 7-2. *Granularity of parallelism*

The CM-2 and the MP-1, on the other hand, are best pro-grammed as fine-grained machines. They are designed to com-municate efficiently after every few instructions. Although they can be programmed in a coarse-grained manner, the usual model is either medium- or fine-grained parallelism. This is true of most SIMD machines. In fact, because the per-processor memory for the majority of SIMD machines is so small, it would be difficult to program them with a coarse-grained approach.

The intermediate ground is held by shared-memory machines like the Sequent Symmetry 2000. The shared memory allows for some parts of the program to be fine-grained and other parts to be coarse-grained. This enables fine tuning, in which the programmer begins with a coarse-grained program and then incrementally turns the slower, coarse-grained parts into a high-performing fine-grained program. Because of the speed of the shared memory in synchronization and communication, it is possible to develop a program that is almost as fine-grained as that of a SIMD machine. As discussed in Chapter 2, the cost of synchronization is free for SIMD machines, but for MIMD machines there is always at least a small cost involved.

One of the big differences among parallel processors is the extent to which existing applications can be used unchanged. The challenge is writing a program (or modifying an existing one) that can take advantage of a particular parallel processor. The following section covers the two main parallel programming models: data partitioning and function partitioning.

Approaches to Parallel Programming

It turns out that many applications naturally exhibit parallelism. Let's take a look at how a program can be parallelized.

For example, to process the payroll for a large company, there might be a number of steps involved, such as preparing a personnel file to extract employee data, preparing and sorting a file of timecard information, and then processing the two files to generate the paychecks. The first two steps can be done in parallel, while the third step needs to wait for the first two steps to complete. Figure 7-3 shows how this might be represented, where dependencies between the tasks are indicated by arrows. In a multiprocessing machine, it is feasible to specify in the job control language that the first two tasks can be executed con-

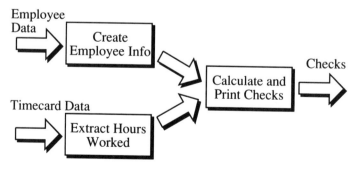

Figure 7-3. *Three-task payroll job,*
showing the dependencies between the tasks

currently, while the third must wait for the completion of the first two. Even a one-processor computer can do processing of other programs while one program is waiting on some form of input or output, and it can complete the application more quickly (in terms of wall-clock time) than if all of the tasks were executed serially.

Problem solving on a parallel processor is approached with two main styles: *data partitioning* and *function partitioning*. Any application may have combinations of these two styles, but these are the building blocks for parallel programs. Data partitioning means that the same operations are performed simultaneously across a large data set. With function partitioning, the solution is structured as an assembly line, with multiple distinct operations happening at each stage.

Programs can be thought of as a series of transformations on a set of data (Figure 7-4). This view holds whether the program is designed for a sequential or a parallel processor. Both parallel and sequential programs input data and, in some order, convert the input data set, by a series of transforms, into the output data set.

Data Partitioning

Figure 7-5 shows the data partition view, where horizontal slices are made of the program, with each processor taking one of the slices. Data partitioning is perhaps the most common form

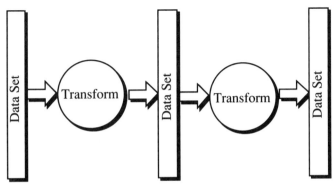

Figure 7-4. *A program as a series of transformations on data*

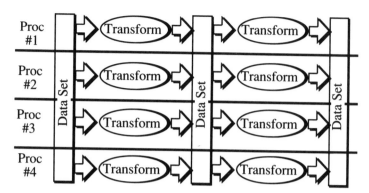

Figure 7-5. *Programming view of data partitioning*

of parallelism. For machines with thousands (or millions) of processors, this style may be the only feasible way of utilizing the processors effectively.

The way it works is that each processor is responsible for performing the transformations on a portion of the data. To carry out the transformations, a processor may need to collect information from other processors, since in a distributed-memory computer, each processor actually has its portion of the data in its own local memory. This means that a synchronization and communication component is added to the transformation.

Example of Data Partitioning

If we look at the payroll example in Figure 7-6, it is obvious that the paychecks for each employee can be computed in parallel. It is conceptually feasible for each employee to be assigned to a particular processor and for all processors to compute the paychecks simultaneously.

To compute a paycheck, each processor needs to hold all of the information relating to a given employee. The processors then sum the hours worked, multiply by the pay per hour, compute the withholdings, and so on. In this example, little communication is necessary between the processors as the computation proceeds.

Function partitioning is usually used for medium- and coarse-grained parallelism. This is because of the complexities in per-

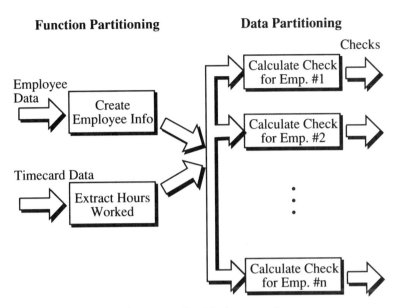

Figure 7-6. *Partitioning example*

forming the necessary communication and synchronization. Figure 7-7 shows how a functionally partitioned program might look. Each of the transformations are meant to be distinct, as opposed to data partitioning, where the transformations are the same.

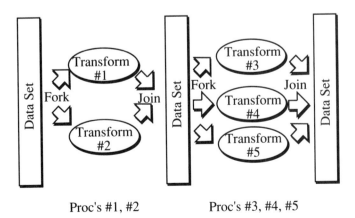

Figure 7-7. *Programming view of function partitioning*

In Figure 7-7, two forms of function partitioning are shown: fork-join parallelism and pipeline parallelism. The *fork* refers to transformations #1 and #2, which can start only after the first data set is available, and they start simultaneously. Likewise, even though the two transformations may end at different times, they reach a synchronization point (they *join*) with the generation of the middle data set. This forking and joining also holds for transformations numbered 3 through 5.

Pipeline function partitioning is realized by the fact that the first set of processors (#1 and #2) can start working on a new data set while processors 3 through 5 are working on transformations 3 through 5, as in an assembly line. In this way, a pipeline of work is created.

Example of Function Partitioning

We can use the same example that was used for data partitioning. In Figure 7-6, the first two tasks, "create employee info" and "extract hours worked," demonstrate a function partitioning, where two different tasks are executed simultaneously.

Languages

From the language point of view, the programmer of a parallel processor has four tools to use:

- Parallel programming standards
- Standard languages that have been extended by the computer vendor, or contain special added libraries, for access to the parallel features of the computer
- Languages designed specifically to express parallelism
- Standard languages and special compilers to find the parallelism in a sequential program

Parallel Programming Standards

Computing standards are everywhere; parallel programming is no exception. Many standards bodies are looking at adding constructs to enable standard languages to be used for writing parallel programs. Most of these constructs allow for only small portions of programs (such as loops) to be parallelized.

These constructs allow the programmer to specify which parts of a program can be executed in parallel and to specify communication and synchronization constraints. This is different from *automatic parallelization,* the ability of a compiler to translate a sequential program into a parallel program with no programmer intervention. Automatic parallelization will be covered later in this chapter.

Not every parallel processor can implement all parallel standards. Different architectures require communication and synchronization to be specified in different ways. What works for one architecture does not work for another. This makes setting standards difficult.

The best example of this is a comparison of two types of machines. A MIMD machine that allows different tasks to execute in parallel, where each processor is independent of the other, can use a language construct that allows the specification of separate, distinct tasks. However, SIMD machines do not have this capability. All parallel tasks must be the same (and must operate in lockstep). The language construct for separate tasks is not useful for SIMD machines. Though a compiler could generate code that runs on the SIMD machine, the efficiency would be less than expected. A SIMD computer would implement the independent tasks serially, not in parallel. This simple example shows how difficult it is to develop a standard parallel programming language that can span architectures with any degree of efficiency.

We will now look at some proposed and existing standards.

Threads
Operating system standards, particularly UNIX, are being established to enable programmers to specify parallelism in the form of *lightweight tasks* (or *threads*). Whereas a *heavyweight* task is usually considered to be composed of thousands of lines of code—and so has a particular overhead structure, which it imposes on the operating system—a lightweight task (more commonly called a thread) is normally much smaller (tens or hundreds of lines) and is designed to create minimal operating system overhead. Heavy-

weight tasks are generally considered to be independent entities with their own files, data, and operating system environment. Threads share files and the operating system environment with their mutual parent, and only their data and subroutine histories are unique.

Multithreading in C

No standard exists for representing parallelism in the C programming language, but several proposed mechanisms have been implemented.[1,2,3] The basic concept is that many threads can operate concurrently.

The C language has always supported the capability to spawn off tasks that have no interaction with the main program. These heavyweight tasks require significant operating system involvement to establish the task. In contrast, a thread is supposed to have significant interaction with other concurrent threads, with minimal startup and shutdown phases. A thread shares data with the main program and other threads; this is how communication takes place.

All of the proposals for adding parallel constructs to C have a programming model of a shared-memory MIMD machine like the Sequent Symmetry. Since there is shared memory, threads must have ways to synchronize access to the shared data. Today, this is contained in special libraries, which are used to augment the C language. In the future, additional language constructs may be added to the C language to support threads more directly, as in Fortran, which is discussed next.

Fortran Parallel Constructs

Fortran 90[4,5] is the latest standard version of the popular language. Since one of the main uses for parallel processing is in the scientific arena, and Fortran is the language of choice for scientists, it makes sense that Fortran is one of the first languages to include parallel processing constructs.

The main parallel processing addition to Fortran involves defining arrays as standard data types, and allowing operations directly on arrays without the need for specifying DO loops. (A DO loop is a looping construct that a programmer uses to specify how to step through an array and operate on each element.) By letting a programmer specify array manipulation at a higher level, the compiler has the opportunity to determine how to compute the operation in a method that is optimal for the computer.

Normally, a programming language can specify operations on simple numbers and characters. For example, most (if not all) programming languages can add single numbers together (such as adding standard weekly pay to overtime earned). However, computing the payroll for a company requires an array that contains entries for each employee's standard weekly pay, and an array with entries for each employee's overtime pay. In the old Fortran language, one could not just add the two arrays together (which in mathematics means adding each element to the corresponding element in the other array). This is because arrays were not elementary data types. In the new Fortran, a programmer can just specify that the arrays be added together and the language will define what that means. The compiler will direct all of the corresponding elements to be added together.

The advantage of this for parallel processors is that a parallel processor can recognize easily that all of the elements of the array can be added together in parallel, and so generate code to cause that to occur.

As shown in Figure 7-8, the program is much simpler in Fortran 90 than in Fortran 77. This simplicity makes the parallelism much

For example, to add two arrays of numbers together (assuming each of the arrays is a 2-dimensional of 100 by 100 elements), the following Fortran 90 program is used:

```
REAL, ARRAY (100, 100) :: A, B, C
A = B + C
```

In Fortran 77, this would have to be done by the following program:

```
  REAL A(100,100), B(100,100), C(100,100)
  DO 10 I = 1, 100
     DO 10 J = 1, 100
        A(I,J) = B(I,J) + C(I,J)
10 CONTINUE
```

Figure 7-8. *Fortran 77 vs. Fortran 90 comparison*

more apparent, not only to the programmer but also to the compiler. The Fortran 90 compiler knows how the array is mapped to the parallel processors (for example, on a SIMD machine each processor might have a part of the arrays) and generates code to optimize the execution. If Fortran 77 were used, the compiler would have a much more difficult time determining the dependencies between the arrays in the DO loop and might not be able to find any parallelism at all.

Extensions and Libraries for Standard Languages

Most parallel processors support standard languages (Figure 7-9), either directly or on the host computer. Standard languages use extensions to access parallelism; some machines have more extensions than others.

Parallel Processor	Main Programming Languages
BBN Butterfly, TC2000	C, Fortran with parallel extensions and library
CM-1, CM-2	C*, *LISP, Fortran 90
iPSC/860	C, Fortran with parallel libraries
Meiko Computing Surface	C, C++, and Fortran, with parallel libraries.
MP-1	MasPar C, MasPar Fortran (based on Fortran 90)
Sequent Symmetry 2000	C, C++, Fortran, and Pascal with parallel libraries, standard multi-tasking in UNIX

Figure 7-9. *Programming languages used by various computers*

Library Routine	Description
m_fork (subroutine)	Starts the execution of the subroutine on other processors
m_get_myid	Returns the process number
m_kill_procs	Stops any processes that have been started with m_fork
m_set_procs	Sets the number of processors that will be used by m_fork
cpus_online	Returns the number of processors in the system

Figure 7-10. *Sample parallel programming library routines*

For example, the Sequent line of parallel processors (discussed in Chapter 4) provides a library of subroutines that the programmer can use to access parallelism. Figure 7-10 describes some of the available subroutines. The programmer simply places calls to the subroutines in the appropriate places in the program. This is certainly the easiest method for supplementing a conventional language with parallelism.

Parallel Languages

As Abraham Maslow said, "To a man with a hammer, the whole world looks like a nail." The tools we use limit the solutions we can imagine. Language is a tool of thought, and programming languages are tools used to describe solutions to problems. A sequentially oriented language makes it difficult to conceive of parallel solutions to problems.

In spite of the extensions to sequential languages discussed in the previous section, there is a general feeling in the parallel processing community that a parallel programming language is needed in order to fundamentally improve the capabilities of programmers to program parallel processors effectively.

Many parallel programming languages have been proposed in the past 20 years. None has actually moved into common production use on a parallel processor. Besides the standard difficulties that any new programming language has in being accepted for common use, these languages also force programmers to think about solutions in very unfamiliar ways. Even if this thinking is beneficial in the long run, the difficulty in learning the approach is a substantial hindrance to the acceptance of the new languages.

The programming language SISAL (Streams and Iteration in a Single-Assignment Language)[6] is representative of a large class of these languages (such as VAL, ID, and Haskell). SISAL is a *functional programming language*. A functional programming language is different from the more common languages in that it is definitional, not imperative. What's more, all of the synchronization and communication is implicit. There are none of the language features for synchronization and communication normally found in other languages, such as locks, barriers, waits, signals, sends, and receives. The programmer simply defines the solution and the compiler infers the necessary parallelism. Functional languages, by definition, express the minimum sequential dependencies.

It will be many years before a parallel programming language is developed that adequately addresses the problem of helping people think of parallel solutions to problems and is still easy to use.

Parallelizing Compilers

The holy grail of parallel processing is the development of a compiler that will take a program written in a standard sequential language (such as C or Fortran) and generate code for a parallel processor such that the program will execute at a high level of efficiency (use 75 percent to 100 percent of the available processors). Developers have been enticed by the fact that vector-processor compilers, which could vectorize many applications, have been around since the early 1980s. It has been assumed that the same type of technology could be applied for parallelization.

SISAL PROGRAMMING LANGUAGE

Development on SISAL began at Lawrence Livermore National Laboratory starting in 1983, in conjunction with Digital Equipment Corporation and Colorado State University at Fort Collins. The goal was to develop a language that would be portable across a wide range of sequential and parallel machines to give users the ability to write complex numerical applications that would naturally take advantage of parallel processors as they became available, without having to rewrite programs for each new machine.

Several large applications have been written in SISAL, and the results have been promising. First, the programs were between one-tenth and one-quarter the size of the applications written in conventional languages. Second, the programs ran as fast as their Fortran equivalents on both vector and scalar shared-memory multiprocessors. And on parallel processors, they scaled almost linearly to take advantage of the multiple processors with no rewrite required.

SISAL compilers exist for a wide range of machines, from the Cray X-MP to the Sequent Symmetry to the CM-2, as well as for experimental parallel processors such as the Manchester Dataflow[7] computer.

Some compilers currently in use do extract some parallelism from "dusty deck" programs. But the parallelism is limited, because the underlying algorithms in the program are generally sequential. The only programs on which a parallelizing compiler can do a reasonable job in detecting and taking advantage of a parallel processor are ones containing looping structures that operate on arrays of numbers.

What is clear is that parallelism requires fundamentally different problem-solving approaches from those typically used in sequential computing. Compilers have not gotten to the level where

---

VECTOR PROCESSORS

A vector processor is a computer such as a Cray-1, that has special operations for doing calculations on vectors of numbers (arrays) very efficiently. For example, the Cray-1 has instructions for adding two 64-element arrays together and hardware that will do this many times faster than if the arrays had to be added one element at a time using a looping structure.

---

they can understand a program and replace sequential algorithms with parallel ones. It is more likely that it will take a new parallel programming language to enable compilers to extract all of the parallelism.

Sequent Symmetry 2000 Programming

Remember that the Sequent Symmetry is a shared-memory MIMD computer. This parallel processor runs the UNIX operating system directly, so programmers interact with it in exactly the same ways that they would with a sequential computer.

Two levels of parallel programming exist in the Sequent Symmetry product family. The first uses the standards-based multiprocessing capabilities of UNIX. Programs that use UNIX-based capabilities for multitasking and interprocess communication run without change and get the advantages of a parallel processor. This accounts for a large number of programs in use today. Client/server application architectures in development are being designed to use these standard mechanisms. They offer coarse-grain parallelism.

The second level of parallel programming is used to make additional performance improvements in applications. At this level, programmers specify the communication and synchronization that must occur between the tasks on the processors. Sequent's Symmetry products provide subroutine libraries for C, C++, and Fortran, which support both data and function partitioning of applications.

Matrix Multiply Example

A matrix multiply easily captures the concept of data partitioning on a Sequent Symmetry. Given two matrices A and B, both of which have 100 rows and columns of numbers, the result of multiplying them together is a matrix C, which also has 100 rows and columns. Each element of C, for example C_{ij}, is created by summing the products of multiplying the ith row of A by the jth column of B.

To data-partition this problem, all the matrices are stored in the shared memory. Each processor is assigned a row of matrix C to compute. Since there may be more rows than processors, and since the processors will not necessarily finish at the same time, each processor will go to a common place and select a row number to calculate. When the processor finishes a row, it goes back and picks another row number, until no row numbers are left. This form of workload distribution is known as the "hungry puppy" method, since each processor hungrily consumes work until there is no more. The pseudocode for this algorithm is shown in Figure 7-11.

What is interesting about the example is that it would be almost the same if it were written for a sequential machine. The only differences are the extra statements to start and stop the processors.

MasPar MP-1 Programming

The MasPar MP-1 computer is a SIMD parallel processor. The machine is actually two computers, but they are well integrated. The front-end computer, on which program development takes

```
program matrix_multiply;
matrix A, B, C [1..100, 1...100];
subroutine multiply_a_row(matrix A,B,C);
  while there are more rows to compute do
    begin
    get a new row number and put it into ROWNUMBER;
    if ROWNUMBER is greater than 100 then
      exit;
    for i starting at 1 up to 100 do
      for j starting at 1 up to 100 do
        C[ROWNUMBER,j] = C[ROWNUMBER,j] + A[i,j]*B[j,k];
    end while loop;
  end of subroutine;

initialize matrix A and B;
start all processors executing subroutine multiply_a_row
(A,B,C,);
wait for all processors to stop;
print out result matrix C;
end program.
```

Figure 7-11. *Matrix multiply pseudocode for the Sequent Symmetry*

place, is a standard sequential computer running UNIX. The parallel processor part of the computer interacts only with programs specially written on the front-end computer.

The MasPar MP-1 has a robust set of program development tools compared to those used for first- and second-generation parallel processors. In the early days, parallel processors were built with fast hardware, no software, and the expectation that users would be so enamored by the performance that they would not mind program development difficulties. The software environment has improved dramatically with the current generation of systems.

There are two approaches to programming the MP-1. The first and most common one is to view the front end and the processor element array as an integrated system and to write one program. The second approach provides the ultimate performance, but requires the programmer to write separate programs for the front end and the processor element array and to be totally responsible for managing the complex interactions between the two subsystems. We will focus on the first approach.

Writing a program for the MP-1 requires the data partition programming model described in Chapter 4. The program is written so that each processor has a part of the data and all processors perform the same operations on their respective parts.

The languages provided for the MP-1 are MasPar Fortran, which is based on Fortran 90, and MPL, a variant of C. Only MasPar Fortran is used for the approach that has one program for both the front end and the processor element array. When MPL is used, the programmer must write separate programs for the two subsystems.

Programming Environment

The program development environment for the MP-1 contains some useful tools for developing and optimizing parallel programs. Much of the investment at MasPar went into software tools to assist in porting and developing large applications. All of these tools are based on a graphical user interface and X-Windows.

The key tools available for the MP-1 are the following:

- A multiwindow graphical user interface
- A symbolic debugger that can simultaneously display and debug what is happening on the front-end computer and in the processor element array
- Browsing tools for managing large applications and their data
- Performance analysis tools to visualize the execution of parallel programs

The performance analysis tools are a huge help in parallelizing a program. By seeing the state of all the processors in a SIMD machine, the programmer can get a much more complete picture of how well the application is taking advantage of the parallel processor and can recognize patterns of execution that can be optimized. For example, one display shows whether each processor is currently executing an instruction or not. (Remember that in a SIMD machine, even though all processors execute the same instruction, the instructions are conditional, and some processors can elect to "sit out" an instruction based on their data.)

Intel iPSC/860 Programming

The Intel iPSC/860 is a distributed-memory MIMD computer. Each processor has its own local memory and executes its own programs. The processors communicate and synchronize by sending messages back and forth.

As discussed in Chapter 4, all program development is done on the front-end computer. Programs are written in C or Fortran and access special libraries that contain subroutines for performing message passing (and access some of the special features of the hardware). The compiled programs are downloaded to the parallel processor for execution. Although it is possible for a programmer to write a program for each processor in the machine (for an iPSC/860 this could be 128 processors!), normally one program is written in a data-partitioned approach and downloaded to all of the processors.

The basic structure of this type of program is identical to that of a sequential program. The difference is that at some point during execution, the program must send some portion of its data to another processor, and it must receive data from other processors. To do this, the special library has subroutines for sending and receiving messages. Note that in a distributed-memory MIMD machine, the data must actually be sent; it is not sufficient to just pass a pointer to the data, because a processor cannot read or write other processors' memories.

Message Passing

Three methods of performing message passing are used in the iPSC/860: synchronous, asynchronous, and interrupt. Each is used in particular programming scenarios to achieve optimal performance and correctly executing programs.

Synchronous Message Passing

Synchronous message passing is the easiest to explain. When one processor needs to send a message to another processor, it stops executing instructions until the message has been moved from its local memory and is placed into the interconnection network (Chapter 4). This is important, because this allows synchronization to occur even when a processor is delayed in getting access to the network. Synchronous receiving means that a processor stops and waits for the arrival of a message that it needs. This means that the processor does no work while it is waiting.

Asynchronous Message Passing

Asynchronous message passing allows processors to continue doing useful work while waiting for a message to be sent or delivered. For example, a processor executing an asynchronous send of a message does not pause for the interconnection network to become available. Instead, it continues executing instructions after the send. The operating system and the hardware are responsible for making sure the message actually gets onto the network.

When a processor has lots of choices of work to do, then an asynchronous receive is optimal. The processor can look to see if a message has arrived without being blocked (stopped). If the message hasn't arrived, then the processor can continue executing other work and just check back periodically to see if the message has been received yet. The processor doesn't have to stop and wait for messages, as it would with a synchronous receive.

Interrupt Message Passing

Interrupt message passing is very similar to asynchronous receives, except the processor does not have to continually check to see if a message has been received; it will be interrupted as soon as the message comes in. When the message comes in, the processor is suspended from doing its normal work and is told to process the message that just arrived. When it has done the processing, it can go back to the work it was doing prior to the message arrival.

Summary

Parallel programming is not nearly as difficult as people thought it was during the early generations. With the two main approaches, data partitioning and functional partitioning, parallel programs can be written fairly concisely.

The most common programming method is to use a standard programming language with special libraries to extend the language to allow access to parallel processor features. New parallel languages are still a long way off. Some of the standard languages, such as Fortran 90, are beginning to add features to allow programs to be portable across a wide variety of parallel processors.

Key Points

1. Parallel programming requires some rethinking of programs, but it does not require complete rewriting.

2. In general, old applications cannot be merely compiled to achieve significant amounts of efficiency on parallel processors. One exception to this is numerically intensive programs.

3. Most parallel processors are programmed using standard languages with some special extensions or subroutine libraries to allow the programmer to explicitly specify the communication and synchronization with other processors.

4. Even though parallel programming languages are widely held to be the optimal approach to parallel programming, it will be many years before a language is developed that provides sufficient development functionality to replace the standard languages.

5. Even though parallel programming today uses high-level languages, the methods of specifying communication and synchronization are equivalent to assembly language programming for parallel processors.

References

1. M. L. Powell, S. R. Kleiman, S. Barton, D. Shah, D. Stein, and M. Weeks, "SunOS Multi-thread Architecture," in *USENIX—Winter '91*, pp. 65–79.

2. F. Armand, F. Herrmann, J. Lipkis, and M. Rozier, "Multithreaded Processes in Chorus/MIX," *Proceedings of the EUUG Spring 1990 Conference,* Munich, Germany, April 1990.

3. E. C. Cooper, R. P. Draves, "C Threads," Department of Computer Science, Carnegie-Mellon University, September 1990.

4. "Fortran 8X Draft," *Fortran Forum,* May 1989.

5. "Fortran 90 Is Technically Complete," *Fortran Forum,* July 1991.

6. J. McGraw, et al. *SISAL: Streams and Iteration in a Single-Assignment Language. Language Reference Manual, Ver. 1.2.* Lawrence Livermore National Laboratory, 1985.

7. J. R. Gurd, C. C. Kirkham, and I. Watson, "The Manchester Prototype Dataflow Computer," *Communications of the ACM,* Vol. 28, January 1985, pp. `34–52.

8

Selecting a Parallel Computer

Once to every man and nation comes the moment to decide,
In the strife of Truth and Falsehood, for the good or evil side.
J. R. Lowell, *The Present Crisis*

Although some companies might still think it risky to base an information system on a parallel processor, it might be riskier not to, given today's extremely competitive marketplace. The evidence in favor of parallel processors is growing as more and more companies successfully make the transition from traditional to parallel systems, thereby gaining a competitive edge. Deciding which parallel computer to purchase is no different from selecting a sequential computer; however, some issues need more thought and attention. They are the amount of future application development, the performance required by the application, the fit of parallel processors to that application, and nonquantitative issues, such as service, reliability, and the operational environment.

Where to Start with Parallel Processing

Companies that have successfully integrated a parallel processor into their information systems (like Kmart and Prudential Securities) have identified critical application areas that clearly benefit from added performance and storage capacities. They have reviewed the strategic objectives of the company and its current information systems and have obtained expert knowledge of the capabilities and weaknesses of parallel processors. The goal is to find an application that is a good fit for the capabilities of a parallel processor and will produce a clear benefit for the company after implementation. This application will guide the development of the benchmarks to be used in the selection process.

Figure 8-1 lists some of the key considerations for beginning parallel processing. Since the investment is nontrivial, and the decision is of a strategic nature—deciding how to move the company further into the information age—senior executives and technical people who understand the company and its fundamental operation in the business world should have major roles in focusing the project and overseeing its implementation.

Since parallel processors have proven themselves already, investigating them should not be viewed as a research effort. It is important to avoid applications that can just as easily be done on more traditional computers, since a company commits to a significant investment in people and time when a parallel processor is brought in.

After the application has been identified, the next step is a preliminary requirements analysis and functional design of the

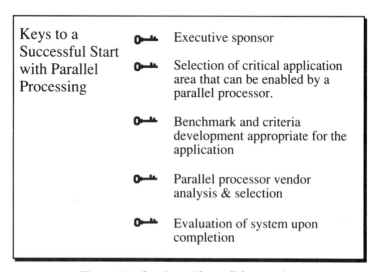

Figure 8-1. *Starting with parallel processing*

Quantitative	☞ Computational Performance
	☞ Memory Capacity (largest applications)
	☞ Mass Storage (total, usable bandwidth)
Qualitative	☞ Interoperability
	☞ Development Environment
	☞ Operational Environment
	☞ Backup
	☞ Reliability
	☞ Service

Figure 8-2. *Important criteria for parallel processors*

information system. This information is then used to help select a parallel processor. Although there are many application development methodologies, the suggested approach is rapid prototyping followed by successive refinements of the application. This is extremely appropriate for new application areas, where little prior experience exists. Because the parallel processor enables a revolutionary step in capability, there will be unforeseen advantages that might not be predictable or possible with a stricter development style.

The rest of this chapter will examine how to select a parallel processor, by looking at the quantitative and qualitative criteria that can have a major impact on the decision (See Figure 8-2).

Quantitative Criteria

So what does one measure when evaluating a parallel processor? The traditional area of performance should certainly be measured, in terms appropriate for the planned applications. Memory capacity is important, because of the lack of virtual memory in many parallel processors and because of performance degradation when an application does not fit in memory (requiring some data to be kept on disk). Beyond that, mass storage capability needs to be analyzed.

Computational Performance

Among the many criteria there is always one which is paramount: how well the computer will perform the job. Determining this for sequential computers is always a challenge; for parallel processors, it is downright difficult. Of course, since parallel computers are naturally scalable, performance is less critical, because the number of processors can always be increased (up to the maximum the architecture allows).

The most obvious area to measure is the computation capability of the machine. In almost all cases, this is the first and primary attraction of a parallel processor and is the most highly touted set of metrics by computer vendors. Computation capacity is the undeniable strength of parallel processors. The goal is to determine how well the computer performs, on the computational side, on the applications you have in mind.

To accomplish this, one would like to program the computer to perform the specific application. That is certainly the most accurate way to determine the answer. This is usually not practical, because the application either needs to be ported to the computer, requiring months of effort, or the application doesn't exist yet and will require years of programming. This means that a computer buyer is left with the alternative of finding a feasible way to measure the computer's performance with something less than perfect. This is typically done with a *benchmark*.

A benchmark is a small program or set of programs that can easily be executed on dissimilar computers to compare them. If the benchmark programs used are representative of the applications that will run on the computer, then the results will be fairly accurate. They work well for sequential computers; as long as the benchmark is written in a language that exists on each computer, then porting is straightforward. But for parallel processors, this is not the case, as we have seen in the earlier chapters.

Since each parallel processor is fundamentally different, the optimal algorithm to execute the benchmark is different for each computer and must be rewritten. This is a time-consuming activity and opens the question of whether the results are comparable.

▼

TRADITIONAL MEASURES OF PERFORMANCE—MIPS, MFLOPS, AND MOPS

The most common metrics for computers are MIPS (millions of instructions per second), MFLOPS (millions of floating-point operations per second), and MOPS (millions of operations per second). Each of these measures a very primitive performance characteristic, which is far enough removed from application performance to be less than useful.

MIPS is the number of instructions a computer executes in one second. For a parallel processor, this is the count of the number of instructions a single processor can execute in a second times the number of processors in the system. This does not take into account the type of instructions (simple adds or complex conditional branch instructions) or the fact that the processors may execute on differing quantities of data. An Intel iPSC/860 can operate on 64-bit data items, while the Thinking Machines CM-2 operates on one bit of data at a time. Also, synchronization and interprocessor communication are ignored in this metric, even though they are the two most important features of a parallel processor (discussed in Chapter 2). Still, if one parallel processor is a hundred times faster in MIPS than another, chances are that it will run the real application faster. However, a factor of two (or even five) may not signify a substantial difference on the real application.

MFLOPS is the number of floating-point additions that the machine can perform. This is a carryover from the early days of parallel processing, when parallel processors were considered applicable only to scientific applications. This metric counts only serial floating-point operations. The number is always the number of MFLOPS for a single processor times the number of processors in the system. It doesn't take synchronization and communication into account. Some processors are tuned so that their MFLOPS rating is actually four to five times the performance of their MIPS rating, but using this comparison for non–floating-point-intensive applications is highly suspect.

Sometimes instructions actually perform more than one operation; in parallel processors, a data item may also be exchanged with another processor in the system while an instruction is executing. Since MIPS and MFLOPS undercount the performance in each of these cases, the MOPS metric was created. MOPS counts the maximum number of operations a processor can perform in a second and multiplies it by the number of processors in the system. Like the previous two metrics, MOPS is overly optimistic on achievable performance.

Parallel processors have an additional constraint. Because of synchronization and communication, not all the processors will be active at any one time. As we have seen with the SIMD class of parallel processors (Chapters 4 and 7), programming can temporarily turn off some processors, so that not all processors participate in all calculations. Using these common metrics to measure parallel processor performance is like measuring the top speed of a car by considering only the engine's RPMs without taking into account transmission gear ratios, wheel diameters, horsepower, aerodynamics of the car, weight, number of passengers, and so on.

Even the computer science community views these metrics with skepticism. In some circles, MIPS stands for Meaningless Indicator of Processor Speed, and MFLOPS are called "macho flops."

Benchmarks

In order to compare parallel processors based on their performance, the user needs to characterize the applications that will be running on the parallel processor. By determining the type of applications that will run on the computer, the user will be able to select or create benchmarks that can yield a meaningful comparison.

Standard benchmarks are those that are in common use throughout the industry (Figure 8-3). It would be nice if most

Benchmark	It Models	Good for These Applications	Endorsed by Standards Body?
Whetstone	Fortran programs	Engineering and scientific applications	No
Dhrystone	System programs	Operating systems and student programs	No
TPC-A	Simple banking transaction, client and server	Online transaction processing	Yes: Transaction Processing Council
TPC-B	Simple banking transaction, server only	Online transaction processing	Yes: Transaction Processing Council
SAXPY	Array multiplication	Certain scientific applications	No
Linpak	Linear algebra subroutines	Many scientific applications	No
SPECmark	Scientific workstation usage	Numerically intensive C and Fortran single user environments	Yes: System Performance Evaluation Cooperative

Figure 8-3. *Common benchmarks*

benchmarks had been blessed and audited by standards bodies, but that is too much to ask. These benchmarks are typically found in the literature supplied by the vendor or in the trade press. Common benchmarks include Whetstone, Dhrystone, SPEC, LINPAK, SAXPY, and the TPC (-A, -B, -C) series. If these apply to your applications, then they are valuable. However, the odds are that most standard benchmarks are meaningless for your applications.

Whetstone and Dhrystone

The Whetstone and Dhrystone[1] benchmarks measure more than simply single instruction speeds. Both fall into the category of synthetic benchmarks (discussed later). They are designed to represent instruction sequences commonly found in certain scientific and business applications. The Whetstone benchmark represents scientific applications (specifically, Fortran programs involving significant matrix calculations). These are heavily, but not solely, floating-point calculations.

The Dhrystone benchmark was created in the early 1980s as a way to measure system program performance. It is not representative of applications, but rather operating systems and other systems-oriented programs. It includes integer calculations, string manipulation, and some data structure accesses, but few (if any) floating-point operations.

As with all metrics, Dhrystones are used and quoted well outside their applicable domain. The Dhrystone has become a common metric for microprocessor and workstation performance.

When applied to parallel processors, it must be remembered that neither metric takes into account synchronization or communication. Both metrics are calculated by using a single-processor number and multiplying by the number of processors.

Neither metric works well for most sequential processors, and neither will help a commercial user determine the appropriateness of one parallel processor over another.

TPC Benchmarks

The widely quoted benchmarks used for parallel processors are the TPC benchmarks,[2] which measure database performance, and the Linpak benchmark, which pertains to scientific programs that are linear algebra problems.

The TPC benchmarks were developed and blessed by the Transaction Processing Council, a group composed of most of the hardware and software companies that are actively involved in online transaction-processing applications. Examples of these are airline reservation systems, bank transaction systems, and order-entry applications.

Two TPC benchmarks exist today: TPC-A and TPC-B. Both are designed around a simple banking transaction, depositing and withdrawing funds from a bank account. The TPC-A benchmark models both the database server that processes the transaction as well as the user (client) side, modeling the screen interactions. The TPC-B benchmark only models the database server side of the transaction.

Other benchmarks are under development by the TPC. They include benchmarks for typical business applications (such as order entry), decision support applications, and complex data management (documents, objects, and records).

TRANSACTION PROCESSING
PERFORMANCE COUNCIL (TPC)

The TPC was founded in 1988 as a nonprofit corporation to define benchmarks for the transaction-processing and database industry and to make these available and widely used by the information-processing community.

The TPC has grown from the original eight members to 43 by the end of 1991. These members include major hardware and software vendors who serve the information-processing industry.

Part of the role of the TPC is to publish specifications that define and regulate the execution of the benchmarks and how the benchmark results are reported. This helps ensure that comparisons between different machines using these benchmarks are valid.

Source: TPC Press Backgrounder, Shanley Public Relations, 1991.

One of the unique elements of the TPC benchmarks is their requirement for auditing. Results of the benchmarks must be audited by a third party to confirm that all rules were followed. These benchmarks report not only the total performance of the system (in TPC-As or TPC-Bs), but also the cost of the system to achieve that performance, which even includes five-year maintenance costs. This makes for a very good comparison between computers.

Most MIMD shared-memory parallel processors are capable of use in database applications, consequently, the parallel processor vendors quote this benchmark in their literature. If your application is transaction processing, then the TPC series is a good way to compare machine performance.

Synthetic Benchmarks

Synthetic benchmarks are by far the most useful. Although they require more work up front, they are easier to use for comparing computers. A synthetic benchmark does not do any useful work, but is an artificially constructed program built from statistics of applications. The result is a small, easily ported program that behaves in the same way as the original set of applications.

The Dhrystone benchmark mentioned above is such a beast. It was constructed by taking language statement statistics from several hundred student systems programs and creating a short program with the same statistics. If, for example, a set of programs has, on the average, 30 percent conditional branch statements (for example, IF statements), then 30 percent of the Dhrystone benchmark would be conditional branches.

In constructing a synthetic benchmark, it is important to collect what are called *dynamic statistics;* that is, statistics generated by the actual running of applications. Statements inside a loop, for instance, should be counted as many times as they execute (using real data), and statements that are never executed (error condition statements) should never be counted. In this way, a true profile of the executing application(s) will be generated. The opposite of these are *static statistics,* collected by simply counting statements in source programs. Up until the 1980s, that was the standard way to determine program statistics.

Synthetic benchmarks work well for sequential processors and for parallel processors that share a common programming model and language. If this is not the case (and it seldom is), then a slight variant of this must take place. A synthetic benchmark for a parallel processor should be specified as a pseudocode description of the algorithm steps necessary. This allows the vendor to develop a program that is specific to the computer without any preconceived ideas of the programming model to be used.

To develop this, the statistics should be collected not at the statement level, but at the algorithm level. In any program there are fundamental algorithms, which are used the majority of the time. These should be identified through performance analysis and synthesized to simpler problems. These simpler problems then become the synthetic benchmark.

This is easy if the applications exist. If they don't exist, then the best thing is to find applications that are similar to the one to be created. If this is not possible, then one should fall back to a small model of the application that contains the kernel of the work to be done.

Application Kernels

More accurate than a synthetic benchmark is the use of real application kernels. Many times, applications have a small kernel, usually less than 10 percent of the complete application, that accounts for 90 percent of the execution time. This can be determined by profiling the application, using tools that are available on most computers. This kernel then can be used as the benchmark. One of the ones used for supercomputers is called the Livermore Loops. This benchmark is just a collection of application kernels from many of the most time-consuming applications run at Lawrence Livermore National Laboratory. The compact size of these kernels makes the porting and running of the benchmark on many different computers very easy.

Be aware, though, that for parallel processors, the 90 percent of the application that is not captured in the application kernel can have a serious impact on the performance. This can happen if the nonkernel parts of the program are completely unparallelizable or do not fit the I/O model of the computer. These would then become the bottleneck when running the real application on a parallel processor. This is why a performance benchmark is only one of the metrics that should be used in selecting a computer.

Complete Applications
Certainly the best approach is to have the application in its entirety be used for the comparison. As described above, this is not often practical.

Memory Capacity

A second criterion looks at the largest application on which a parallel processor can effectively operate. As soon as they run out of memory, most parallel processors substantially degrade in performance. For example, if an application requires a cross-correlation on a table constructed of a hundred million customer purchases, but only a million will fit into the memory at a time, then the I/O time required to move data in and out of memory must be included in the benchmark.

What makes this more important is that many parallel processors don't have virtual memory. This means that the hardware and software that have provided traditional computers with seemingly endless amounts of memory, automatically managed with no programmer intervention, is not present. If a program requires more memory than is available, the programmer must write often convoluted code in order to run the application, keeping some of the data on disk and moving to memory when it is needed. Though not impossible, this is a skill that most current-day programmers have never had to develop.

Mass Storage

Usually programs that require lots of computation also need lots of data. There are two metrics for mass storage capability: total directly accessible mass storage and realizable I/O speed. *Directly accessible mass storage* is the total amount of disk that is readable and writable from within a parallel program.

12 WAYS TO FOOL THE MASSES ON PERFORMANCE

1. Use 32-bit arithmetic, not 64-bit arithmetic, for performance benchmarks. Compare 32-bit performance versus competitors' 64-bit performance.

2. Assume that the inner kernel of an application is the sole determinant of application performance.

3. Use assembly code and other low-level language constructs for performance and compare them with others' Fortran or C implementations.

4. Scale up the problem size with the number of processors, but don't clearly disclose this fact.

5. Estimate linear scaling of performance without proof.

6. Compare the performance of heavily optimized benchmarks against unoptimized Cray benchmarks.

7. Compare with an old code on an obsolete system.

8. Base MFLOPS operation counts on the parallel implementation instead of on the best sequential implementation.

9. Give performance in terms of processor utilization, parallel speedups, or MFLOPS per dollar (peak MFLOPS, not sustained).

10. Use algorithms that are numerically inefficient, compared to the best known serial or vector algorithms for an application, in order to show artificially high MFLOPS rates.

11. Measure parallel run times on a dedicated system, but measure conventional run times on a heavily loaded system.

12. If all else fails, show pretty pictures and animated videos, and don't talk about performance.

Source: David H. Bailey, "Twelve Ways to Fool the Masses When Giving Performance Results on Parallel Computers," *Technical Report RNR-91-020,* June 11, 1991, NASA Ames Research Center, Moffett Field, CA 94035.

Realizable I/O speed looks at the software necessary to read and write to the mass storage system. Since performance of an application depends on the speed of the I/O, the I/O needed by the application should be measured, in terms of megabytes or gigabytes, and then a model of the application's I/O should be run to estimate the performance. The model should include more than the total amount of data read and written; it should also cover the distribution of sizes for each read and write, and whether they are sequentially or randomly distributed on the disk.

One area that is often overlooked when benchmarking a parallel processor is the presence of a data hot spot. A *hot spot* is a small amount of data that must be accessed by a large number of processors; for example, an index structure of a database. On sequential processors this is not important, but in a parallel processor, since all of the processors must coordinate their access to the hot spot, the performance can be severely degraded. The performance can be so badly degraded that only one processor at a time is executing, with the others waiting their turn. However, this problem can usually be rectified by a slight modification to the application's algorithm.

Qualitative Criteria

Besides criteria that can be numerically compared with some degree of accuracy, there exist a number of criteria less able to be measured on a rigid scale, but no less important. These should be looked at in comparison to the company's and the application's needs, and compared across the parallel processing vendors.

Interoperability

Four facets exist for interoperability: interconnect hardware, software protocols, performance, and security. The parallel processor must have the necessary hardware interface to connect into the application environment. For the software protocols, the issue again is whether the appropriate software exists to allow the computer to interact in the application environment with other computers.

The performance of the parallel processor in the interoperable environment is more difficult to determine. The ability of the parallel processor to respond to more than one request at a time must be evaluated. This is because even though the computer may have a distinct processing performance, it may not have the necessary software to perform the networking tasks in parallel. An exception to this is the Sequent Symmetry systems with their Parallel STREAMS (see Chapter 4).

Finally, security is a concern in most information systems. For heterogeneous computing environments, this is especially important. Since many parallel processors are placed in client/server applications, it is critical to have some form of security system in place to authenticate users and applications. This applies equally to parallel processors and sequential processors. The advantage a parallel processor may have is that the security software may be parallelizable and therefore provide better performance.

Development Environment

A general misconception is that any computer with as much power as a parallel processor should easily handle program development tasks. It turns out that some parallel processors are better suited to this than others. The Intel iPSC/860 in the case study (Chapter 6), for instance, executed all its program development software on the SRM (essentially a PC), although developers have since ported some software to other workstations. But to support 100 programmers doing application development might require a separate set of computers (including a dedicated parallel processor for application testing).

The best approach to configuring a development environment is to determine the application development methodology and the number of developers, and to work with the parallel processing vendors to create the right configuration.

Operational Environment

The operational environment encompasses two metrics of importance: the number of developers who can be active at any one time and the number of active users. Some parallel processors have a limited application development environment which runs on only a single-processor, or host computer. This limits the number of active developers due to the power of the single processor. It may also turn out that developers cannot use the system simultaneously with applications, or it is very risky for the application if they do.

The number of active application users is also a factor. This is limited by the connectivity of the system as well as how the users are connected. If they have to be connected through a single-processor front end, then the limit will be more severe than if they were connected in some parallel fashion to the computer, with the users distributed over the parallel processors.

Backup

Backup is forgotten most of the time, but when large amounts of storage are involved, backing up data can be very time-consuming. If data has to go through a single host computer over a low-bandwidth network, then backup time may be prohibitive. An example is the early iPSC/860 computers. I/O to the parallelized disks was done through the hypercube network; however, there was no UNIX-controlled backup of the disks. The disks had to be read by the host computer and written to tape one at a time. This did not take advantage of the parallelism and was slow. In current versions, this problem is solved by the addition of tape drives under control of the Concurrent File System, which also manages the disks.

A side issue is whether there is appropriate software to manage the backup tapes. Many early parallel processors ignored this area, assuming a high level of sophistication among operators. In these cases, the solution usually involves sending the data from the parallel processor to another computer over some form of network and having the other computer perform and manage the backup.

Reliability and Service

In general, the reliability of parallel processors is very good. This is in large part due to their use of microprocessors, which drastically reduces the number of parts in the system (thereby increasing the reliability).

One of the areas in which parallel processors excel is in the use of multiple processors to increase the reliability to the level of fault tolerance. One of the big problems with sequential, single-processor systems is that if any part of the machine malfunctions, the computer is nonfunctional.

With a parallel processor (since by their very nature they have multiple hardware components), if one part of the machine malfunctions, it is theoretically possible for the machine to keep running by using some of the redundant parts. An example of such a machine is the Sequoia line of fault-tolerant parallel processors. This machine has up to 32 processors, which work similar to the Sequent Symmetry (Chapter 4). However, the Sequoia computer system has extra hardware and software for detecting and correcting errors. This means that if a processor or memory fails, the system will gracefully recover the application and data and continue to function. At some later point, the failed hardware can be replaced, without even stopping the computer. This extra level of reliability is critical for business applications such as telephone switching, reservation systems, and banking applications.

Most parallel processors that are not fault-tolerant can be restarted and the operating system software automatically will configure the malfunctioning parts offline. This means that the computer is still usable, but with some degradation of performance. This is a fallout of parallel processing.

Summary

The most successful companies are moving quickly to take advantage of parallel processing as a way to be competitive in the information age. To do this, they are developing key applications on parallel processors today.

Selecting a parallel processor is similar to selecting a traditional computer. The differences include benchmarking, which is harder for parallel processors. The application selection and benchmarking process usually need the participation of a parallel processing expert. Qualitative criteria, such as system management software, backup, interoperability, and application development environments also have issues that should be looked at closely when comparing parallel processors.

Key Points

1. Companies should start now to develop applications on parallel processors.

2. Parallel development projects should be sponsored by upper management, because of the strategic impact that parallel processing can have on a company.

3. A key application should be selected for implementation on a parallel processor, and this application should be the basis for the benchmarking.

4. Benchmarking of parallel processors should direct special attention to processor performance, memory size, and mass storage capabilities.

5. Special areas to examine: application development environments and operational environments. Multiuser and multitasking capabilities may be important for particular applications.

References

1. R. P. Weicker, "Dhrystone: A synthetic systems programming benchmark," *Communications of the ACM*, vol. 27, no. 10, October 1984, pp. 1013–1030.

2. Jim Gray, ed., *The Benchmark Handbook: For Database and Transaction Processing Systems*, (San Mateo: M. Kaufmann, 1991).

9

The Future of Parallel Processing

To boldly go where no one has gone before.
Opening lines to *Star Trek: The Next Generation*

The future for parallel processing looks bright. As the world's economy changes from manufacturing to information,[1] parallel processing will be there, enabling companies to be more competitive than ever. We have seen how and why parallel computers came into being and how they can be put to use by major corporations. Here we will look at some of the recent events that occurred as this book was being written and at some of the applications that can be created because of parallel processing.

Computing Will Change

It's difficult to see the value of a traditional sequential computer, especially one that is not based on microprocessors. The most likely scenario is that in the next 5 to 10 years, minicomputers and mainframes, as we now know them, will disappear. Companies will be using parallel processors like the ones described in this book as the main computational and storage elements in consolidated information systems in order to gain competitive advantages. Information systems will become real-time; that is, decision makers will be able to know the state of their businesses at any point in the day.

Single-processor machines will exist only on the desktop. The performance of microprocessors is increasing at a phenomenal rate, nearly doubling every year. At this rate, by 1995 a single microprocessor will perform as well as a 1988 Cray Y-MP (single-processor), and there are no physical barriers to prevent performance improvement. With that much computational power, the desktop will be a combination of images, graphics, voice, and text.

What will not be on the desktop is servers: computation servers, information servers, storage servers, and so on. These will all be parallel processors. It is difficult to predict how large these may become. Since individual microprocessors will be in the 250-MIPS range in 1995, how many processors will be in the larger parallel machines? In announcements at the end of 1991, computer vendors were anticipating machines with tens of thousands of processors in 1992. By 1995, will that number be in the hundreds of thousands?

The Next Mountain

Given large increases in computational power and storage capacity, what is next? In the past, as computers became faster and faster, there were always applications waiting to take advantage of the improved machines. The era we are now in is different from before. The power unleashed by parallel processors is not just an evolutionary advance, a factor of two or four; it is a revolution. In 1990, industry analysts were talking about reaching a teraflop (one million million floating-point operations per second) by 1995; by the end of 1991, that performance level was expected during 1992. This opens up tremendous doors. Conceiving and developing the applications is now the bottleneck. Companies that can do it have demonstrated huge competitive advantages.

One of the next hurdles is developing tools that can integrate the information and speed application development. Among the approaches that are being tried, *object-oriented programming* (OOPS) seems to be showing significant promise, and OOPS maps well onto parallel processors (Chapter 4). Another promising area is hypermedia, which is just beginning to come out of the research labs and become part of advanced information systems.

A concurrent challenge is high-speed networking. Proposals at the national level[2] champion the creation of an *information highway*, an electronic interstate highway system. The intent is to provide the infrastructure necessary to support an economy based on information—the information age. This network would transmit data at over 1 gigabit per second; fast enough to transmit all of the data in an encyclopedia in under 4 seconds, fast enough to transmit the largest corporate databases that now exist in less than a half hour.

After a network like this has been put into place, demand for parallel processors will be even greater. When the huge amounts of information that now reside on publicly accessible computers are networked with this information highway, the competitive advantage will lie with those who can use it effectively. Searching through voluminous quantities of information to find something valuable—*information mining*—is one major emerging use of parallel processors.

Information Applications for the Future

The following are some information applications that are enabled by parallel processing. They would not be possible without the power and storage of these new machines, and each can provide a substantial competitive advantage.

Securities Trading

As we have seen in the case study on Prudential Securities (Chapter 6), the use of parallel processors on Wall Street has already begun. Prudential uses its parallel processor for analysis of collateral-backed mortgage obligations and now also does real-time monitoring of each trade to determine risk exposure. Other financial firms are starting to investigate parallel processing, looking for ways to provide faster in-depth stock analyses for their traders.

Customer Service

A major part of customer service requires sorting through lots of information to come up with specific answers to customers' questions. In most companies, this information is spread across a multitude of databases, filing cabinets, desks, and regional service centers around the world. It is not uncommon for a customer service representative to have multiple terminals connected to multiple computers. Because of its complexity, the search for an answer can be quite time-consuming and frustrating for impatient customers.

These obstacles to providing prompt customer service are caused in large measure by the lack of technology for merging information into a single entity, allowing for different data formats (such as images, text, and voice notes), and providing quick search times.

Parallel processors can remedy this situation. The latest systems, combined with the latest information management software, can drastically improve response time. Online storage of huge amounts of information is not a problem, and such systems are currently being networked to user-friendly front ends. Reducing customer service response times makes for happier customers and saves substantial amounts of money.

Retailing

One of the biggest collectors of data is the ubiquitous barcode scanner, that tracks every item sold at stores across the nation. Companies sort and sift through this information to some extent, but usually not on a daily basis, and certainly not completely. This vast information reservoir holds the key to product buying patterns and emerging trends and, combined with census data and other purchaser information, can reveal an incredible amount about what products sell and why.

Processing this information in real time (or even daily) requires a high-performance data communications network for collecting the raw data and a parallel processor to store and analyze it. Performing associations and calculations on billions of pieces of data would be simply out of the range of even the most advanced sequential computer.

Imagine being able to correlate coupon advertisement to actual buying patterns and being able to target mailings only to customers who would use products or respond to offers. The savings from the additional knowledge are endless.

On the production and distribution side, real-time barcode information would allow a company to apply just-in-time processes to the distribution and stocking of retail stores. By knowing what and where items are selling, as well as the trends, companies can keep just the right quantities at each store. And when this information feeds into production planning systems and business simulation (discussed later), the companies can maintain a near-perfect balance among their resources.

Corporate Archives

Think of the paperwork that crosses your desk daily. Multiply that times the number of days you have worked for the company. Do that for all of the employees in the company. Add in other information like product design documents, faxes, articles in the company newsletter, and presentations. The amount of information is overwhelming. All of that work has been done and paid for. It represents, to a large degree, the assets of the company.

What information is locked away in that storehouse? When an employee leaves a company, think of the information that is lost. How many times have you gone through the files of former employees uncertain about what to do with this or that piece of paper? Not only is one individual's knowledge irretrievable, but so is part of the company's information asset.

Now, put a parallel processor in the company as an information server in place, a repository for all of this information. Allow people to browse through terabytes (1000 billion bytes) of information in seconds, to search for answers to questions, scan old faxes, or check on early presentations to customers to see what was really presented and committed.

Corporate Competitor Tracking

The world is moving faster and faster. Events that can affect your business are not happening just down the street or even across the country, but they are taking place around the world. It's impossible to keep track of events without help.

Parallel processors are being put to use to track the news and continuously search for information that is important to a company. Prototypes of these systems are in use today, but are limited to a few news sources and have a limited search capability.

The ideal system would be continuously gathering information from all news sources around the world. It would translate all news into a common language. It would scan for topics that an executive has specified; whenever news relating to any of the specified topics occurs, the system would email or fax a copy of the information to the requestor. It would also be able to store online news from five, 10, or even 20 years ago, allowing a search to pinpoint patterns and trends that might be important to a business.

Such a system will be based on parallel processors, which have the storage capacity (Teradata computers can already hold terabytes of data), the performance (Intel's Paragon performs at 160,000 MIPS, or 10 Cray Y-MP C90s), and the networking capability (Sequent's Parallel Streams technology allows network performance to scale just like processors).

Business Strategies

One of the more promising applications of parallel processing is in business simulation. Today, scientists in almost all disciplines are using computers to simulate physical processes, dramatically reducing the time it takes to get data and conducting experiments that can't be done in the physical world. The result is an explosion of knowledge in the sciences.

Imagine being able to simulate a business and continually refine the simulation with a real-time information system, enabled by parallel processors. Simulations like these allow executives to experiment with business decisions. For example, if orders for new goods rise by 10 percent, a simulation can predict the impact on the number of personnel in the company, and where staffing should be increased for maximal efficiency.

In the years to come, a new field will blossom in business and information systems, bringing the mathematics of physical simulations to business modeling.

OIL EXPLORATION

For many years, oil exploration has been a computer-intensive business. Oil companies have exploited the fastest computers available. The problem is a combination of huge volumes of data and the need to perform complex numerical analysis on that data. For seismic modeling, data is collected from both small-scale explosives and thumper-trucks on land and on explosives in the ocean. The data, often in the tens of gigabytes, is brought back to a processing center, where it is examined. In the past, data accumulated so fast that many thousands of reels of computer tape went unanalyzed.

But in 1989 a major breakthrough occurred. At Mobil Research, a seismic modeling application was run on a 64,000-processor Thinking Machines Corporation CM-2. The application, including all of the I/O, achieved a sustained performance of 5.6 GFLOPS (5.6 billion floating-point operations per second). This production application is so fast that it actually computes the results twice as fast as the data is collected. No more backlogs!

This application won the 1989 Gordon Bell Prize in performance, which is awarded yearly in recognition of "outstanding achievements in the application of parallel processing to scientific and engineering problems" for the application "running faster than any other comparable engineering or scientific application." This prize is awarded by the editors of *IEEE Software Magazine*.[3]

Mobil Oil Corporation has also announced that they will be taking delivery of a new CM-5, one of the first to be shipped.

Source: Jacek Myczkowski, Doug McCowan, and Irshad Mufit, "Finite-Difference Seismic Modeling in Real Time," *Geophysics: The leading edge of exploration,* June 1991.

Product Development Time Reductions

Even though product development time is outside the domain of information systems in most companies, it is worthwhile to mention, as it can have a dramatic impact on the bottom line.

All product development, no matter what the industry, is a cycle that includes multiple iterations of designing, prototyping, and testing. These are very time-consuming. In the physical sciences, scientists are already using supercomputers (and more recently parallel processors) to simulate an experiment rather than conduct it. This saves tremendous time, and in some instances it is not even possible to perform the test physically, due to safety precautions.

Historically, the use of supercomputers has been too expensive to use the same techniques of simulation for product development. But parallel processors, with their significant price advantages over traditional supercomputers, are changing that. The latest generations of parallel processors are less expensive by several factors than a traditional supercomputer, while also being several times more powerful. The result is that companies will start developing the capability to reduce their product development time by one or more iterations, not only saving money but, more importantly, achieving a faster time to market.

Summary

We are at the beginning of a massive change in the information strategies of corporations. The information age is upon us, and parallel processors are part of the key to winning. It is a revolution.

References

1. Shoshana Zuboff, *In the Age of the Smart Machine: the Future of Work and Power*, (New York: Basic Books, Inc., 1988).

2. "Creating A Great Computer Highway," *New York Times*, September 2, 1990.

3. J. Dongarra, A. H. Karp, K. Kennedy, and D. Kuck, "1989 Gordon Bell Prize," *IEEE Software*, May 1990, pp. 100–110.

Glossary

"The question is," said Alice, "whether you *can* make words mean
so many different things."
"The question is," said Humpty Dumpty, "which is to be
master—that's all."
Lewis Carroll, *Through the Looking-Glass*

AMDAHL'S LAWS   A set of conjectures first stated by Gene Amdahl
(one of the designers of the IBM System/360) which relate the
performance of a computer to memory size and I/O bandwidth.
Thought to represent a balanced system for general-purpose
computing.

APPLICATIVE PROGRAMMING   A programming model in which the
fundamental operation is the application of mathematically defined functions to data.

BENCHMARK   A program that measures the performance of a computer, especially to compare the performance of two or more
computers.

CACHE   High-speed memory designed to hold recently used
memory data. Used to increase the performance of computers.

CACHE COHERENCY   A mechanism to keep the caches in a multiprocessor system in agreement, so that two caches don't hold
different values for the same memory location.

COARSE-GRAIN PARALLELISM   A program in which the parallel processors communicate and synchronize infrequently, normally
only after thousands of instructions.

CONCURRENT   Occurring in the same time frame; said of two or more activities in a computer. The activities are not necessarily simultaneous; instead, the processor can be taking turns executing one activity and then the other.

DATAFLOW   A form of parallel processing in which instructions (or subroutines) execute as soon as the data they need is available.

DHRYSTONE   A benchmark program used from the mid-1980s onward to measure the performance of a computer on system programs. Used most often with workstations and minicomputers. *See* Whetstone.

DISTRIBUTED MEMORY   A type of parallel processor architecture in which each processor has its own memory which other processors cannot read or write.

EMAIL   Electronic mail; the sending of electronic documents from computer to computer through a network. The networks can be public as well as private.

FINE-GRAIN PARALLELISM   A program in which the parallel processors communicate and synchronize frequently, normally every few instructions.

FUNCTIONAL PROGRAMMING   A programming model related to lambda calculus, in which variables can be assigned a value only once.

GRAND CHALLENGE   A scientific problem which, if solved, can significantly move a scientific discipline forward. The government (DARPA) has listed 20 grand challenge problems that use computers as part of the expected solution path.

HIERARCHICAL DATABASE MANAGEMENT SYSTEMS   A database in which relationships between data items are described by fixed pointers, in a hierarchical fashion. This limits the number of relationships that can be described.

HOT SPOT   An area of data that must be accessed frequently by many processors in a multiprocessor system. When this occurs, the effective performance of the multiprocessor is severely degraded.

HSC   High-Speed Channel, an I/O interface used mainly with supercomputers.

HYPERCUBE NETWORK   A common method for interconnecting parallel processors, based on the geometric concept that each of 2^n processors is a corner in an n-dimensional cube, and the edges of that cube are the direct connections between processors.

INFORMATION MINING   Searching through huge amounts of data, such as documents, newsletters, electronic mail, and so on, to extract new knowledge and information.

LINPAK   A set of programs used in scientific applications for performing linear analysis, used to benchmark scientific-oriented computers and supercomputers.

MASSIVELY PARALLEL   A type of computer that uses hundreds or thousands of processors to solve a problem.

MEDIUM-GRAIN PARALLELISM   A program in which the parallel processors communicate and synchronize about every 100 instructions.

MESH NETWORK   A method for interconnecting parallel processors. A mesh is like the wires on a screen, in which processors are placed at the junctions of horizontal and vertical wires.

MFLOPS   Million floating-point operations per second. A measure of performance used in comparing computers that do scientific calculations.

MIMD   Multiple instruction-stream, multiple data-stream. A class of parallel processors in which each processor executes a different program on different data from other processors. Pronounced "mim-dee."

MIPS   Millions of instructions per second. A measure of computer performance that counts the maximum number of instructions a computer can execute. Analogous to measuring the speed of a car by the number of rotations the tires make in a hour.

MULTICOMPUTER   One style of parallel processing, in which each processor is essentially a small computer with its own memory and I/O capability.

MULTIPROCESSING One style of parallel processing that can be executed on sequential computers, in which multiple independent programs can execute simultaneously, or at least concurrently.

MULTIPROCESSOR Any computer with more than one processor. Normally used to denote parallel processors with less than ten processors. As the number of processors increases, this term is used less frequently.

NETWORK DATABASE MANAGEMENT SYSTEMS A database in which the relationships between data items are described by fixed pointers, but in an arbitrary fashion. This allows more relationships to be described than a hierarchical database does.

OPEN SYSTEMS A computer or software system based on standards, so that components of the system can be purchased from multiple vendors.

PARALLEL PROCESSING The use of more than one processor to execute a single application.

PROPRIETARY PROCESSOR A processor with an instruction set that is available from only one computer vendor.

RELATIONAL DATABASE MANAGEMENT SYSTEM A database in which the relationships between data items are described by tables which can be constructed at any time. There are no fixed pointers that describe the relationships.

SHARED MEMORY In a multiprocessor, a memory location that is accessible from any processor in the system.

SIMD Single instruction-stream, multiple data-stream. A class of parallel processors in which all processors execute the same instruction simultaneously, but on different elements of data. Pronounced "sim-dee."

SIMULTANEOUS In computers, refers to two or more things happening at the same instant.

SUPERLINEAR Parallel-processor performance that grows faster than the number of processors predicts. For example, a superlinear four-processor system might exhibit performance greater than four times that of the one-processor system. When performance is measured and compared properly, superlinearity cannot occur.

SUPERSCALAR   A style of processor construction in which a single processor can execute more than one instruction from an instruction stream at a time.

TP-1   A measure of a computer's database performance, replaced in the late 1980s by the TPC benchmarks.

TPC   The Transaction Processing Performance Council, composed of hardware and software vendors and users with interests in online transaction processing. Sponsors standard benchmarks for evaluating hardware and software for transaction processing applications, the TPC-A and TPC-B benchmarks.

TPS   Transactions per second. A measure of performance of a computer system. A transaction is a complete database operation: a retrieval, storage, or update of a record in a database. For example, a user making a withdrawal at a bank initiates a single transaction that updates his or her bank account.

WHETSTONE   A benchmark program used in the 1970s and early 1980s to measure the performance of a computer on scientific applications. *See* Dhrystone.

Appendix A

Directory of Companies in Parallel Processing

Advanced Computer Research Institute (ACRI)
1 Boulevard Marius Vivier-Merle
69443 Lyon Cedex 03
FRANCE
Phone: 33 72 35 84 00

Building a parallel processor supercomputer with high single-processor performance oriented toward scientific and technical markets. First shipments are expected in the mid-1990s.

Active Memory Technology
16802 Aston Street
Suite 103
Irvine, CA 92714
Phone: (714) 261-8901

The DAP/C8 is a SIMD parallel processor with up to 4096 one-bit processors. The application focus is on scientific and defense uses. The DAP/C8 comes in commercial and embedded packaging.

Alliant Computer Systems
1 Monarch Dr.
Littleton, MA 01460
Phone: (508) 486-4950

The Campus/800 is a massively parallel distributed-memory MIMD computer oriented toward scientific applications.

ARIX
821 Fox Ln.
San Jose, CA 95131
Phone: (408) 432-1200

The System90 Series is a family of shared-memory MIMD multiprocessors oriented toward online database applications. The systems can have from one to six main processors and up to 20 I/O processors.

Compaq Computer
20555 FM 149
Houston, TX 77070
Phone: (713) 370-0670

The SystemPro is a small shared-memory MIMD computer with one or two processors. Its main use is as a server on a PC network.

Corollary, Inc.
2802 Kelvin Ave.
Irvine, CA 92714
Phone: (714) 250-4040

The 386/smp and 486/smp systems are shared-memory MIMD computers with up to ten i386 or i486 processors, respectively. The systems support 64 MB of memory. The I/O is through standard PC I/O cards. These products are bringing parallel processing to the PC world.

Cray Computer Corporation
1110 Bayfield Dr.
Colorado Springs, CO 80906
Phone: (719) 579-6464

The CRAY-3 is a 2–16-processor vector-oriented supercomputer. First shipments are expected during 1992.

Cray Research, Inc.
608 2nd Ave.
Minneapolis, MN 55402
Phone: (612) 452-6650

The YMP-C90 is a 16-processor vector-oriented supercomputer. A massively parallel computer based on the DEC Alpha microprocessor is expected to be available sometime in 1993.

Encore Computer Corporation
6901 West Sunrise Boulevard
Fort Lauderdale, FL 33313
Phone: (305) 587-2900

The Infinity 90 series consists of shared-memory MIMD computers focused on information system applications. The systems can have from 1 to 800 processors.

Intel
Supercomputer Systems Division
15201 NW Greenbrier Parkway
Beaverton, OR 97006
(503) 629-7835

The iPSC/860, a distributed-memory MIMD computer with up to 128 processors, is the low-end parallel processor from Intel. The Paragon is also a distributed-memory MIMD computer, but it has a faster interconnect. The Paragon can have up to 4000 processors.

Kendall Square Research Corporation
170 Tracer Lane
Waltham, MA 02154
Phone: (617) 895-9400

The KSR1 is a shared-memory MIMD computer with from 16 to 1088 processors. It is designed to support scientific and engineering applications as well as online transaction processing and relational databases.

MasPar
749 North Mary Avenue
Sunnyvale, CA 94086
Phone: (408) 736-3300

The MP-1 is a SIMD parallel processor with up to 16,535 processors. Its focus is on scientific and engineering applications.

Meiko Scientific
1601 Trapelo Road
Waltham, MA 02154
Phone: (617) 890-7676

The Computing Surface is a distributed-memory MIMD computer that scales from 2 to greater than 100 processors (theoretically unlimited). The focus is on scientific and engineering applications.

NCR/Teradata
101 North Sepulveda Boulevard
El Segundo, CA 90245
Phone: (213) 524-6162

The DBC 1012 Model 4 is a distributed-memory MIMD computer that works as a database server to a host computer or a network. The system can have up to 1000 processors and over 4 terabytes of online storage. The machine is not generally programmable.

nCUBE
919 E. Hillsdale, Suite 200
Foster City, CA 94404
Phone: (415) 593-9000

The nCUBE 2 parallel processing computer system is a distributed-memory MIMD machine with up to 8192 processors. It is focused on scientific applications and recently on large-scale relational databases.

NetFRAME Systems Inc.
1545 Barber Lane
Milpitas, CA 95035
Phone: (408) 944-0600

A family of network servers is focused on providing file services, server-based applications, and network management for PC networks. The higher-end systems in the family offer from 1 to 10 processors in a shared-memory MIMD configuration. The multiprocessors provide a level of fault tolerance as well as performance enhancement.

Pyramid Technology Corporation
3860 N. First Street
San Jose, CA 95134
Phone: (408) 428-9000

The MIServer S series is a shared-memory MIMD computer focusing on the online transaction processing (OLTP) and relational database marketplaces. The MIServer Reliant series also are shared-memory MIMD computers, with high-availability features such as redundant hardware and software which provide approximately three-minute recovery times after hardware or software faults. The systems scale from 1 to 24 processors (only 12 in the S series).

Sequent
15450 SW Koll Parkway
Beaverton, OR 97006
Phone: (503) 578-5700

The Symmetry 2000 series of shared-memory MIMD computers is focused on commercial information system applications. The systems can have from 1 to 30 processors.

Sequoia
400 Nickerson Rd.
Marlboro, MA 01752
Phone: (508) 480-0800

The Sequoia Series 400 systems are shared-memory MIMD machines with a high level of fault tolerance. The machine scales from 1 to 32 processors. The primary application areas are those environments that demand fault tolerance.

Silicon Graphics
2011 N. Shoreline Boulevard
Moutain View, CA 94043
Phone: (415) 960-1980

The IRISservers are shared-memory MIMD computers with a focus on high-performance file servers for networked environments. The IRIS 4D/GXT series computers are shared-memory MIMD computers focused on visualization, scientific, and engineering applications. Both computers support one to eight processors.

Solbourne Computer, Inc.
1900 Pike Rd.
Longmont, CO 80501
Phone: (800) 676-5268

The Series 700 departmental server and the Series 5E/900 enterprise server are shared-memory MIMD computers, with up to four or eight processors, respectively. Both are oriented toward database and engineering applications.

Stratus Computer, Inc.
55 Fairbanks Blvd.
Marlboro, MA 01752
Phone: (508) 460-2000

The XA/R series are shared-memory MIMD computers which are focused on fault-tolerant online transaction processing. The multiple processors are used for both performance and fault-tolerance.

Sun Microsystems
2550 Garcia Avenue
Mountain View, CA 94043
Phone: (415) 960-1300

The Sun SPARCsystem 600MP is a family of shared-memory MIMD multiprocessors designed for file server environments. The high-end system can have up to four processors.

Thinking Machines Corporation
245 First Street
Cambridge, MA 02142
Phone: (617) 234-5525

The CM-5 is a distributed-memory MIMD machine with up to 16,535 processors (currently SPARC microprocessors), oriented toward scientific applications. Recently, some machines have found use in information-intensive applications.

Torque Systems, Inc.
700 High Street
Palo Alto, CA 94301
Phone: (415) 321-1200

The ComputeServer is a distributed-memory MIMD machine with 1 to 64 processors. Focus is on computation-intensive problems of electronic CAD, three-dimensional graphics, prepress imaging, and financial analytics in a network environment.

Others Designing or Selling Parallel Processors

- Concurrent Computer Corporation
- Digital Equipment Corporation
- Fujitsu
- Hitachi Data Systems
- Hewlett-Packard
- IBM
- International Parallel Computers
- Parasys
- Siemens-Nixdorf
- Suprenum (Germany)
- Tera Computer
- Unisys

Index